HARVARD EAST ASIAN MONOGRAPHS

25

THE ROAD FROM ISOLATION

THE CAMPAIGN OF THE AMERICAN COMMITTEE

FOR NON-PARTICIPATION IN JAPANESE AGGRESSION

1938–1941

THE ROAD FROM ISOLATION: THE CAMPAIGN
OF THE AMERICAN COMMITTEE FOR NON-PARTICIPATION
IN JAPANESE AGGRESSION, 1938-1941

by

Donald J. Friedman

Published by the
East Asian Research Center
Harvard University

Distributed by
Harvard University Press
Cambridge, Mass.
1968

The East Asian Research Center at Harvard University
administers research projects designed to further
scholarly understanding of China, Korea, Japan, and
adjacent areas.

Preface

The Japanese seizure of the Chinese province of Manchuria in 1931 initiated the ten-year chain of aggression that was to lead to the United States' abrupt entrance into the Second World War and finally to her membership in the postwar United Nations. During this troubled period the American people radically readjusted their conception of the role of the United States in the community of nations.[1]

For the larger part of the prewar decade, the United States sought security in isolationism, in the loosening first of political ties and then of economic ties with foreign lands. America's long tradition of non-involvement in the affairs of the world, which for most of her history meant the affairs of Europe, was reinforced by the impact of the Great Depression, which encouraged a spirit of intense economic nationalism in the United States as well as in Europe. More importantly, historical American isolationism was revitalized by the contagion of aggression which spread from Manchuria to Ethiopia and eventually to Western Europe itself. As both Europe and Asia degenerated into a state of war, Americans almost unanimously retreated into their own hemispheric dream world. The full-blown isolationism that had resulted by the mid-1930's was more pervasive, more aggressive than any of its predecessors. So strong was this wave of emotion that as powerful a leader as President Franklin D. Roosevelt, an internationalist at heart, did not dare to oppose it for the first years of his administration.

Yet, even while this tide of isolationism was gaining in momentum, a small number of Americans looked beyond their

v

seemingly impregnable fortress and saw that the events of
Europe and Asia could not be viewed with detachment; they
perceived that America might not be able to preserve her
heritage or even her very existence as an independent
nation if bellicose totalitarianism were to replace freedom
and democracy in other regions of the world. These people
remained mere voices in the wilderness until October 1937
when President Roosevelt called them forth to do battle
against their isolationist opponents.

The storm that his "Quarantine Speech" then raised
induced Roosevelt to back down rapidly from the implications
of his analogy; but, nevertheless, his address marked the
beginning of the end for this phase of American isolationism.
The transition toward the assumption of a more responsible
role in international affairs was far from rapid; by Pearl
Harbor only a very small minority of the American people
understood the full extent of the overseas commitments which
the United States would have to make in order to realize her
goal of a world of peace, justice, and prosperity. Three and
a half years of devastating warfare were required before the
mass of Americans came to support extensive international
cooperation as reflected in the nation's membership in the
United Nations.

Perhaps the most arduous phase of this evolution of
attitude was the initial period in which the majority of
the American people were wrenched from their fantasy land
of isolationism and were forced to focus their attention on
the bitter realities of the world of the late 1930's. Once
this first step had been taken, every additional move was
made just a little bit easier. Because it represents such
a critical turning point in America's international perspective, this reawakening of America's active concern for
a free and democratic world is an epoch of particular interest
to the historian.

During this prewar period scores of private pressure groups were operating in the field of foreign affairs, all propounding a specific program for American policy. They ranged in their approaches from the anti-interventionist stance of America First to the internationalist one of the Committee to Defend America by Aiding the Allies. Likewise, their attitudes toward the government ran the gamut from intimate cooperation to acrimonious opposition.

Many of the more influential of these organizations have been made the subjects of historical monographs, probably the finest of which is Professor Wayne S. Cole's *America First: The Battle Against Intervention, 1940-1941.*[2] One of these groups, however, has not been the object of any serious study and, as a result, has been relegated to an undeservedly obscure role in accounts of the period.

The American Committee for Non-Participation in Japanese Aggression carried on an intensive and ambitious campaign from August 1938 to February 1941 to remove the economic support which America was giving to the Japanese military for its brutal expansion in China, which had begun in the summer of 1937. In terms of the extent of its efforts, the committee had few if any rivals until the emergence of the Committee to Defend America and the America First Committee in the middle of 1940.

In one sense, this book is simply a chronicle of the activities of an important yet relatively unknown organization; but, in another, more important sense, it is a study of the early stages of the evolution of American thought from isolationism to international·involvement. Although the role of the committee in this development is difficult to assess, there is considerable reason to believe that it was significant. Its program was an important element in overcoming the indifference and isolationism

both in the public at large and in the government with regard
to America's part in the Sino-Japanese conflict. In addition,
since America's involvement in Asia in the prewar years
preceded and to some degree facilitated her involvement in
Europe, the efforts of the committee helped to effect changes
in America's foreign policy in regions other than the Far
East. Thus, this little-remembered group may have played
a crucial and even unique role in the rebirth of America's
active participation in world affairs.

This study has been based primarily upon an examination of the manuscript records of the American Committee for
Non-Participation in Japanese Aggression at Littauer Center
of Public Administration, Harvard University. This investiga-
tion of the committee's archives has been supplemented to
an extensive degree by correspondence and interviews with
several members of the group, particularly with its executive
secretary, Harry B. Price. Since Mr. Price has read the
entire manuscript and has commented upon every aspect of
it, the author has thought it best, in the interest of
brevity, to footnote only those statements which may seem
obviously interpretative or controversial.

The writer was introduced to the archives of the
committee during his final year at Harvard College, by his
tutor, James C. Thomson, Jr., who provided invaluable
assistance, especially in preparing an earlier draft of
this study for submission as a senior honors thesis in
history. While these and others were consulted, they may
not agree with every point in this text. In any case, the
final responsibility for this book lies solely with the
author.

Donald J. Friedman

December 1967

CONTENTS

Chapter I

FORMATION

Although the invasion of China had begun in July
1937, it was not until the following spring that trade
statistics revealed the extent to which the United States
was supplying Japan with essential war materials. In the
months that followed the release of these statistics, several
scholars analyzed the figures, reporting their findings
in the press.

The well-known economist, Eliot Janeway, wrote two
of the most prominent of these articles; they appeared in
the June editions of *Harpers* and *Asia* magazines. He reported
that one-third of the steel Japan made in 1937, steel for
shells, bombs and bullets, came from American raw materials.
Seventy-five per cent of the gasoline Japan used that year,
gasoline for tanks, bombers and warships, came from the
United States. Altogether, the United States had supplied
54.5 per cent of Japan's entire import of munitions and
munition supplies, including some crucial items such as high-
grade steel, machinery and lubricating oils which she could
not have obtained elsewhere.[1]

When these magazines came out on the newsstands in
late May, they created a minor sensation among China's many
friends in America, especially in the New York City area. One
of these friends was Harry B. Price, a lecturer in economics
on leave from Yenching University in China.

Harry Price had been born in China in 1905, the son
of a famous Southern Presbyterian educational missionary.
After spending much of his youth in and around Nanking, Price

came to the United States to attend Davidson College in
North Carolina, where he received his baccalaureate degree
in 1925. After graduation from college, he worked and studied
for two years at the University of Missouri and then worked
briefly for the Western Electric Company in New Jersey.
Returning to China in 1929, Price served as Assistant to the
American Commission of Financial Experts to the Government
of China. He soon came back to the United States to earn his
master's degree in economics at Yale University in 1932. The
same year Price once again returned to China to teach at
Yenching University in Peiping, the leading private university
in China, founded in 1870. He served as an instructor, then
lecturer in economics and after 1935 as Acting Dean of the
College of Public Affairs. Two weeks before the Sino-Japanese
War began, Price completed a five-year term and returned with
his wife and two small children to the United States.[2]

After reading Janeway's articles, Harry Price discussed
them with his brother the Reverend Frank W. Price, an educational missionary with a wide reputation for his efforts toward
reconstruction in rural China, who was then on furlough from
the Nanking Theological Seminary. Together, they decided
to invite to an informal meeting several New Yorkers who they
felt would be interested in investigating ways of stopping
America's support of Japan's war of aggression in China.

In the last week of May 1938, the Price brothers
called a meeting of several such men in Harry Price's Manhattan
apartment. Prominent within the group was Dr. B.A. Garside.
Born in Stringtown, Oklahoma, in 1894, Dr. Garside had taken
his undergraduate degree at the University of Oklahoma and
his master's degree in Educational Administration at Teacher's
College, Columbia University. From 1922 to 1926 he had
served as an educational missionary in China, first at a middle

school in the Presbyterian Mission in Weihsien, and later at
Cheeloo University in Tsinan. Returning to the United States
in 1926, Garside served as Secretary of the China Union
Universities Central Office and as Executive Secretary of
its successor, the Associated Boards for Christian Colleges
in China. It was in connection with his work in the Associated
Boards that Dr. Garside met Harry Price.

Present also at the first meeting was Dr. Edward
H. Hume, a graduate of Yale University and of Johns Hopkins
Medical School, who had served for over twenty years as a
medical missionary in China. In 1938 he was Director of the
China Medical Council for Overseas Work, a clearing house
for medical missions.

Philip J. Jaffe, managing editor and part owner of
Amerasia, a periodical specializing in Far Eastern affairs,
also attended this first gathering. In addition to his
interest in *Amerasia*, Jaffe was the owner of a large Christmas-
card company in New York City.

Jaffe invited to this meeting Thomas Arthur Bisson,
a member of the editorial board of *Amerasia* and a Far Eastern
authority on the research staff of the Foreign Policy Association.
Born in 1900, Bisson had received his B.A. from Rutgers and
his M.A. from Teacher's College, Columbia University. From
1924 to 1928 he had served as a missionary teacher in China,
first at Han Mei Middle School in Hwaiyuen, Anhwei, and later
at Yenching University in Peiping. Since 1928 most of his
time had been spent with the Foreign Policy Association and
with writing his authoritative account of Japan's aggression
in China, *Japan in China*.

The final member of the original group was Earl H.
Leaf, a writer and former North China manager of United Press,

who was then engaged in public information work for the Chinese Nationalist Government. A young, outspoken man, Leaf already was friendly with most of the people at this first meeting.

Many years later Harry Price recalled the composition of this original gathering:

> It was a diverse group, some of whom might never have met each other but for a strong common, immediate concern over the extent to which the American economy was, in fact, providing large resources to the ambitious military clique leading Japan in an unprovoked military aggression against China.[3]

At this first meeting the group considered the programs and policies of existing organizations interested in political action in foreign affairs. After finding that none of these was completely suitable to the task, it decided to investigate the possibility of creating a new committee for the specific purpose of stopping American support of Japan's aggression.

In the series of meetings that followed in late May, June and July the membership of the group grew, and the purpose of the as-yet-unnamed committee became more closely defined. To realize the goal of curtailing America's support of Japan's military machine, at least two broad methods were available: an embargo of exports of essential war materials to Japan, and restrictions upon imports of goods from Japan. Early in their planning, the group decided to concentrate upon the first method, the embargo, primarily because most felt that the stoppage of the export of war supplies would be a more vivid, more direct issue which would elicit more public support. Also, a group was already working toward a consumer boycott of Japanese goods, whereas

there was no such group working primarily toward an embargo.
Finally, this boycott group, the Committee for a Boycott Against
Japanese Aggression, was strongly leftist, at least in the
eyes of the public; and leaders of the new committee recognized
the liabilities of too close an identification with a leftist
organization. Even after a study by several members revealed
the importance of American imports to Japan--these imports
provided Japan with the foreign exchange needed to purchase
many of her essential war supplies[4]--the group continued to
concentrate its efforts upon an embargo on the export of war
materials.

The subject of a name was raised during one of these
early conferences. Several possibilities were discussed,
but the only one that was felt to convey accurately and precisely the goal of the committee was uncomfortably long.
Better long than misleading, said Harry Price, whereupon
the group tentatively adopted as its name "The American
Committee for Non-Participation in Japanese Aggression."
This emphasis upon precision rather than sensationalism
proved to be characteristic of the committee's activities
for the next two and a half years.

In early June before the organization was formally
established, Harry Price traveled down to Washington to
sound out the attitudes of Administration and Congressional
leaders toward the proposed campaign. On June 7 Price talked
with Stanley K. Hornbeck, formerly Chief of the Far Eastern
Division and then Chief Advisor on Far Eastern Affairs in
the Department of State. Hornbeck encouraged the idea of
an educational campaign that would bring significant facts
to the attention of the American people. He noted that public
opinion was apathetic toward the situation in Asia. Hornbeck,
who was to become the committee's closest contact within the

State Department, hoped that the group could help to break down the isolationist temper of the American people. On the same day Price also met with Dr. Charles Moser, an economic advisor in the Department of Commerce, and John Carter Vincent, an advisor in the Division of Far Eastern Affairs of the Department of State, both of whom stressed that the committee, to be successful, must base its appeal firmly on American interests.[5]

On June 8 Price talked with several Congressmen including Senator Key Pittman, chairman of the Senate Foreign Relations Committee, who expressed hope that the group could educate the American people to take a sterner view of Japan's unwarranted aggression. Returning to New York, Price reported to his associates that he had found a number of government leaders, especially in the State Department, who favored the formation of such a group, under responsible leadership, to build up public support for a stronger stand against Japan's expansionist policy.[6]

With this encouragement the committee moved to expand its organization. It approached a public relations firm, Perry and Wise, which submitted a long-range plan for the organization and methods of the group.[7] Although this plan was not adopted, partly because of its cost--Perry and Wise asked $1000 per month for professional services--the committee was later to act upon several of the report's preliminary suggestions.

During the months of June and July, many new members were added to the young organization: Eliot Janeway, author of the articles which had precipitated the group's formation, Edgar H. Rue, executive secretary of the Institution for the Chinese Blind, a philanthropic organization based in New York,

Josephine Schain, national chairman of the National Committee
on the Cause and Cure of War, a coordinating body for eleven
women's organizations such as the League of Women Voters
and the American Association of University Women, George A.
Fitch, a secretary of the Young Men's Christian Association
in China, and his wife Geraldine, Major Evans F. Carlson,
former United States military attaché in China, Maxwell
Stewart, a former educational missionary at Yenching University, who was then associate editor of *The Nation*, editor of
Public Affairs Pamphlets and chairman of the American Friends
of the Chinese People, and Professor Reinhold Niebuhr of the
Union Theological Seminary.

At this stage of the committee's development, its
membership consisted largely of people who had had direct
contact with China in an educational, medical, missionary,
philanthropic, or diplomatic capacity. There also was a
sprinkling of New Yorkers interested in foreign, especially
Asian, affairs.

Beginning in the middle of June, members of the
committee started to work on a brochure in which it would
state the case for American non-participation in Japanese
aggression. The greater part of the booklet *America's Share
in Japan's War Guilt* consisted of quotations from government
officials, newspaper editors and columnists, church leaders
and others condemning Japan's ruthless attack upon China and
deploring America's supporting role. In a ten-page section
in the middle of the pamphlet, there was a series of questions
and answers dealing with the issue of non-participation in
Japanese aggression. After including excerpts from Janeway's
two articles and a similar one by T.A. Bisson, the booklet
ended with a description of the objectives of the committee.

The group, it was said, would help in crystallizing public
demand and support for governmental action to check the flow
of American war credits and war materials to Japan. As had
been agreed in the first meeting of the group, its goal was
defined in limited terms: "The central and single aim of the
Committee is expressed in the phrase 'non-participation in
Japanese aggression.'"[8]

During this period in June and July, the committee,
aided by Harry Price's wife Elizabeth, approached over seventy
organizations and publications to invite their assistance
and to secure a composite list of many thousand individuals
to whom complimentary copies of *America's Share in Japan's
War Guilt* would be mailed. On August 1, 1938, 22,000 booklets
were sent to every Senator and Representative, and to many
foreign policy groups, universities, key people in churches,
organizations interested in China, Rotary, Kiwanis and other
clubs, women's and peace organizations, and other agencies;
and the committee made a public announcement of its formation.[9]

At this stage of its organization, the committee had
a National Board, which consisted of twenty-one early members;
but day-to-day operating decisions were largely made by a
small group consisting of Harry Price, Dr. B.A. Garside, T.A.
Bisson, Dr. Edward H. Hume and Josephine Schain. Frank Price
was active only during the first weeks of the committee's
existence since he was not living in New York; by October
1938 he had returned to China, and his only connection with
the committee thereafter was through correspondence with his
brother.[10] Earl Leaf, another initial member of the group,
dropped out voluntarily at the beginning of September so that
no one would jump to the erroneous conclusion from his official
connection with the Chinese Information Service that the

committee was in any way prompted by or linked with the
Chinese government.[11]

In the National Board meeting of July 27, 1938, it
was agreed that Harry Price, as committee secretary, should
send to the members for approval the names of those who had
been suggested as sponsors.[12] These sponsors simply would
be people who had subscribed to the principle of an embargo
on war materials to Japan and were willing to have their
names used in the committee's announcements. No other participation was required of them. Early sponsors included such
people as Dr. Robert E. Speer, former president of the Federal
Council of Churches of Christ in America, Dr. A. Lawrence
Lowell, President Emeritus of Harvard University, Paul H.
Douglas, professor of economics at the University of Chicago,
and Helen Keller, the famous author and lecturer. By January
1939 the committee had compiled a sponsor list of fifty-three
names including prominent people in the fields of education,
religion, journalism, the arts, business and politics.[13]

Beginning in the middle of September, the National
Board discussed the possible selection of an active chairman
for the committee.[14] Harry Price, as secretary, had general
administrative and executive responsibility for all matters
of the organization; but in order to build up the prestige
of the committee, the members hoped to secure the services of a
chairman who could concentrate upon relations with influential
citizens and with Washington. For two months the committee
debated possible names, but none of the men whom they approached
could take the job. Finally, in mid-December the board decided
upon the selection of Roger S. Greene, a member of the committee
since July.

Greene was a mature, dignified man with many important

connections in Washington. He had received his B.A. from
Harvard in 1901 and his M.A. in the following year. Immediately afterwards he had entered the United States Con-
sular Corps; for the next eleven years he was stationed in
Brazil, Japan, Siberia, Manchuria, and finally China. After
1914 Greene had become involved in the Rockefeller Foundation,
serving as director of its China Medical Board, vice-president
in the Far East of the Foundation, and finally acting director
of the Peiping Union Medical College. Through his work in
the Rockefeller Foundation, Greene had met several members
of the then non-existent committee, including Harry Price.
Although he had recently moved to Chicago in order to work
with the World Citizens Association,[15] he kept in constant
contact with the national headquarters in New York through
a voluminous correspondence with Price.

To assist Greene, the committee secured Josephine
Schain to act as vice-chairman and as treasurer, Mrs. Sidney
D. Gamble, wife of a wealthy New York sociologist who had
specialized in studies of Chinese rural life and was then
president of the Princeton-Yenching Foundation. Price
remained as executive secretary, continuing to exert active
leadership in the organization.

Shortly before Greene had been asked to be chairman,
the committee had approached Henry L. Stimson to serve as
its honorary chairman. For several months it had been
planning to take this step, but the board decided to wait
until the organization had been functioning for several months
and had built up some momentum before approaching Stimson.
There was virtually no disagreement within the group as to
the choice of Stimson. Already over seventy-two years old,
Stimson had served as Secretary of War under President Taft

and as Secretary of State under President Hoover. As Secretary
of State, he had recommended a firm policy toward Japan
after her invasion of Manchuria in 1931, issuing his famous
"non-recognition" doctrine. His reputation by 1938 was such
that his name was literally a household word; the committee
felt that he was by far the best choice for the position.

After Stimson had discussed the program of the committee
with Greene, Price and Hume, Price on December 16, 1938, wrote
Stimson inviting him to become honorary chairman. In his letter
Price mentioned the possibility of asking Dr. Speer and
Dr. Lowell to serve as honorary vice-chairmen if Stimson
accepted.[16] In his reply Stimson did agree to accept the
position, but only if the committee first could secure the
acceptances of these two men. Immediately, the group approached Speer and Lowell as well as William Allen White,
a leading figure among American publishers and editor of
the *Emporia Gazette*. By Christmas Day of 1938, these three
men had accepted; and when informed of this news, Stimson
gladly consented to serve as honorary chairman.

On January 19, 1939, the committee publicly announced
the completion of its organization under the leadership of
Stimson, Speer, Lowell and White.[17] The same evening it
secured its fourth honorary vice-chairman, Jonathan W. Daniels.
Daniels, the liberal editor of the *Raleigh News-Observer*,
had a wide reputation throughout the South; the committee
chose him primarily for geographical distribution but also
for his prominence in the field of journalism.

With the addition of Daniels, the organization of
the committee was essentially completed. In the next two
years of operation, it greatly expanded its membership and
leadership but along the lines established in January 1939.

To handle the growing business of the organization, two more
active officers were added: Dr. B.A. Garside, one of the
original members, became a vice-chairman along with Josephine
Schain, and Mrs. Grover Clark, widow of a noted authority
on the Far East, became corresponding secretary. Two more
honorary vice-chairmen were added in November 1939: Admiral
Harry E. Yarnell, U.S.N. (ret.), former commander-in-chief
of the United States Asiatic fleet; and Henry I. Harriman,
a leading businessman and former president of the United
States Chamber of Commerce. The National Board expanded
to twenty-nine members, adding such people as Dr. Walter H.
Judd, a returned medical missionary from China, whose extra-
ordinary speaking talent proved to be one of the committee's
greatest assets, E. Snell Hall, Frederick C. McKee and A.
Merle Hooper--all prominent businessmen, Chase Kimball, a
banker and director of the National League of Nations
Association, and Ellen Auchincloss, former American secretary
of the China Mass Education Movement. The list of sponsors
swelled to eighty-six, broadening to include unofficial
representation drawn from many diverse influential groups
in American life.

Chapter II

ORGANIZATION AND CAMPAIGN

Even after the organization of the committee had
been completed in January 1939, it remained a group of strong
individuals, operating within a relatively loose organization.
As T.A. Bisson recalls: "my memory is of many like-minded
people joining where and when they could their *individual*
actions to the general objective of divorcing American exports from the Japanese war machine."[1] It became a principle of operation that whenever possible members should
continue to work through their customary channels, using
the medium of the national office only when needed. This
decentralization was stressed partly in order to preserve
and foster a kind of spontaneity that would have a deeper
effect upon the government and upon the public at large than
if an obviously organized series of releases were given out
solely by an agency whose function was to promote the embargo.
But, also, the informality of operation was a necessary result of the nature of the membership of the committee. The
wide range of personalities and political outlooks encompassed
within it could not have been contained within a strict organization; most of its members would not have functioned
either willingly or effectively within a disciplined frame-
work.

At the top of the committee's organization were its
honorary officers: the honorary chairman Henry L. Stimson
and the six men who at one time or another served as honorary
vice-chairmen--Dr. A. Lawrence Lowell, Dr. Robert E. Speer,

William Allen White, Jonathan W. Daniels, Henry I. Harriman
and Admiral Harry E. Yarnell. Stimson, though not holding
public office at the time, was heavily occupied in his law
practice as well as in a personal campaign to educate the
American people and government to take a more responsible
role in international affairs.[2] Remaining aloof from the
ordinary business of the committee, he still consulted frequently on matters of policy with Price or Greene, wrote a
fund-raising letter in his own name, and attended several
luncheons with important citizens in his capacity as honorary
chairman. The primary contribution of the honorary vice-
chairmen was the use of their names to enlarge the reputation
and prestige of the committee, except for Admiral Yarnell
who repeatedly gave valued advice and help.

A second phase of the committee's honorary leadership
was its lengthy sponsor list. Beyond the lending of their
names, the contributions of these sponsors ranged broadly.
At one extreme were sponsors like Mrs. George A. Fitch, wife
of a secretary of the Young Men's Christian Association in
China, who went on several speaking tours for the committee,
appeared before a Congressional committee investigating
revision of the Neutrality Act in May 1939, wrote numerous
articles dealing with America's policy in the Far East, and
carried on an extensive correspondence with the committee's
officers in New York and Washington. At the other extreme
were sponsors like Paul H. Douglas, then professor of economics
at the University of Chicago, whose only correspondence with
the committee was his letter accepting the invitation to
become a sponsor. More typical than either of these extremes
were sponsors like Henry P. Chandler, president of the
Chicago Bar Association, whose participation in the organization's work included writing a short statement supporting

the embargo which was circulated among lawyers by the committee.

The committee's third source of advisors was its un-official members, men who for one reason or another preferred not to become publicly identified with the group. Henry Luce, editor of *Time, Life* and *Fortune,* never became a sponsor but repeatedly discussed the organization's activities with Price or Garside and attended a committee-sponsored luncheon honoring Stimson. Frederick V. Field, secretary of the American Council of the Institute of Pacific Relations, chairman of *Amerasia,* and executive secretary of the American Peace Mobilization, was unable to become officially connected with the committee because his position in the Institute of Pacific Relations prohibited such affiliation; but he often discussed the com-mittee's progress with Price, contributed anonymously--by his request--to its operation, and attended several National Board meetings with the stipulation that his attendance not be recorded.[3] Other friendly, unofficial counselers included Edward C. Carter, secretary-general of the Institute of Pacific Relations; Dr. James T. Shotwell, director of the Carnegie Endowment for International Peace; and Dr. Edward C. Lobenstine, chairman of the Rockefeller-supported China Medical Board.

The official leadership of the committee lay in the hands of its National Board, a group of twenty-nine prominent men and women willing to take an active role in the affairs of the organization. The National Board met on the average of about once every other month, but sub-committees of the board met more frequently. The National Board approved the broad policies of the committee, while permitting its officers a wide range of discretion in working toward agreed objectives.

The work of the committee was conducted mainly by its active officers. Roger S. Greene served as chairman,

16

but Greene himself stated: "by far the most important share in this enterprise has been taken by Mr. Harry B. Price, our Executive Secretary, my real service having been mainly as assistant to him."[4] Since for nearly all of 1939, Greene was living in Chicago and for most of 1940, in Washington, he was physically separated from the national headquarters and was forced to rely extensively upon correspondence, especially with Price.

The national headquarters of the committee was located in an office building in mid-Manhattan. Under the leadership of Harry Price, the headquarters at its height employed nineteen full-time and five part-time employees.[5] The active vice-chairmen, Josephine Schain and Dr. B.A. Garside, maintained close contact with the office, played leading roles within the Board, and were continuously consulted. The treasurer, Mrs. Sidney Gamble, related to the Gambles of the Proctor and Gamble Company, provided broad financial supervision; an accountant within the office, Muriel FitzGibbon, handled the details of the committee's financial affairs under Price's direction. Mrs. Grover Clark, as corresponding secretary, was in charge of much of the group's correspondence, especially that with cooperating committees. The other staff members in the national headquarters included research workers, public relations specialists, and secretaries.[6]

As committee members found themselves traveling more and more frequently down to Washington, the National Board decided on January 3, 1940, to establish a permanent office in Washington.[7] Three days later Greene resigned his position with the World Citizens Association in Chicago and took charge of the committee's new Washington office.[8]

Working with one secretary, Greene kept the national headquarters in New York closely informed of the situation in
Washington. He actively interviewed and corresponded with
a considerable number of Administration and Congressional
leaders as well as with executives of national organizations
whose headquarters were in Washington. Greene also arranged
appointments, from time to time, between other committee
members and various government leaders.[9]

Stanley K. Hornbeck, chief advisor on Far Eastern
Affairs in the State Department, was the committee's closest
contact within the Administration. Consulted by Price before
the organization of the committee was officially announced,
Hornbeck received all of its reports and often discussed
its plans, sometimes critically, with Price and Greene.
Although Hornbeck kept his independent position, was properly
detached, and never hesitated to challenge the assumptions
or disagree with the views of the committee, Price always
knew that he was basically friendly. Hornbeck was willing,
the members of the group believed, to transmit its views
frequently to Secretary of State Cordell Hull.[10]

Maxwell Hamilton, chief of the Far Eastern Division,
was also consulted often by members of the group, but he did
not appear to be as much in sympathy with their views as
Hornbeck. Secretary Hull himself was interviewed on several
occasions by Price and Greene; each time Hull registered
approval of the committee's educational efforts. Although
Greene tried more than once, he could not secure an appointment
with President Roosevelt.

In addition to the Administration leaders, several
Congressional leaders had frequent contact with the committee.
Senator Key Pittman, chairman of the Senate Foreign Relations

Committee, had been consulted by Price during his trip to
Washington in June 1938, and he had numerous talks with Greene
and Price during the next two and a half years. He received
all of the committee's literature as well as some assistance
from its members when considering proposed legislation to
block the export of war materials to Japan. Leaders in the
organization also spoke on several occasions with Senator
Lewis B. Schwellenbach, the author of another embargo bill.
At one time or another, members of the committee talked to
scores of other Senators and Representatives, sometimes
seeking their detailed views on issues relating to the embargo.

Relations of the committee with many members of the
Administration remained generally friendly. From the point
of view of many leaders in the Administration, the committee
was serving an essential purpose by helping to generate
popular sentiment conducive to a firmer American stand on
the Far East. Hornbeck commented repeatedly on the effectiveness of the committee in bringing the situation to public
attention. He looked upon it as a major factor in overcoming
the indifference and isolationism which were impeding the
growth of support for the firmer policies that he believed
were needed to curb the aggressiveness of Japan's military
leadership.[11] Secretary Hull emphasized to Greene that the
agitation of the group was "an essential element in the
situation,"[12] and to Price he said that it was very important
that the group continue its efforts.[13]

From the point of view of the committee, a cooperative
relationship was the most effective way of securing results.
From the beginning of their efforts, its officers sought to
avoid alienating the very people in the government who were
in the best positions to exert positive leadership. Also, a

majority of the committee felt that to pursue a more caustic line toward the government would be to risk the support of many of its more influential leaders. Greene cited an additional reason for prudence and moderation when he remarked, in regard to Stimson: "If...Stimson accepts the honorary chairmanship, I believe that it will be necessary also to take special precautions to avoid embarrassing him by any of our statements or actions."[14]

A minority within the committee urged that in its correspondence and literature the committee criticize freely the "failure" of the Administration; but the majority generally resisted such demands.[15] On one occasion Mrs. George Fitch proposed picketing the State Department, but her suggestion was never considered by the officers of the committee.[16] Roger Greene opposed a more severe policy toward the State Department even though he once confided that he felt that "Secretary Hull is far too timid a man and too lacking in decision to be Secretary of State at this time."[17]

By August 1938 when the organization of the committee was formally announced, it had already established contact with over seventy different organizations. In its expanding contacts with these and other groups, the committee sought to avoid being excessively influenced by any other agency. It solicited and accepted the cooperation of these many organizations on the one issue of non-participation in Japanese aggression, but refused to be identifed with their more extensive programs.

The closest contacts were developed with the American Union for Concerted Peace Efforts. The American Union had on its executive board members of a majority of leading peace organizations, including the National Committee on the Cause

and Cure of War, the League of Nations Association, the Church
Peace Union, and the American League for Peace and Democracy.
The director of the American Union, Dr. Clark M. Eichelberger,
became one of the committee's earliest sponsors. Likewise,
Price became a board member of the American Union and with
Josephine Schain, already a member, succeeded in gaining for
the non-participation program top priority on the American
Union's list of active objectives.[18]

In August 1939 Greene proposed to Price that the
committee consider merging with the American Union;[19] but
Price argued that a merger would involve the committee in
the less clear-cut, more diffuse issues of the American Union,
would risk dissipating the energies of the committee in the
broader program of the American Union, and would alienate
several present supporters of the committee.[20] Although this
merger never occurred, the committee continued to remain on
intimate terms with the American Union.

The National Committee on the Cause and Cure of War,
a clearing house for eleven non-isolationist women's organizations interested in peace, headed by Josephine Schain, also
stressed the non-participation issue in its program.[21] Of
the twenty-one members of the Executive Board of the National
Committee, six eventually became National Board members or
sponsors of the American Committee for Non-Participation in
Japanese Aggression.

The committee did not become actively linked with
the American League for Peace and Democracy, another prominent
peace organization. It felt that it could not risk close
contacts with leftist groups such as the American League.
As Price remarked on November,1938, he hesitated to link
the name of the committee with the American League, which was

"branded by a good many as being 'red' and 'communistically dominated.'"[22] It became a policy of the committee not to have its name officially connected with any function of the League, though it did not try to prevent a few members from participating occasionally as individuals in these affairs.

A similar policy prevailed with regard to another apparently leftist organization, the American Friends of the Chinese People.   Although the chairman and treasurer of the American Friends--Maxwell Stewart and Edgar H. Rue, respectively--as well as a few members of its National Advisory Board were National Board members of the Non-Participation Committee, the committee initially avoided overly close contacts with the American Friends or with its magazine *China Today*. As Greene commented privately, "...when our work began the latter organization [American Friends] was very much under communistic influence and it seemed better policy to keep somewhat aloof from it."[23] However, as the leftist influence within the American Friends appeared to decrease in strength, the committee's relations with it became less guarded.

Although this prewar period in the United States may be contrasted with the postwar period in that liberals and leftists sometimes were more able to work together toward specific goals, especially in the international field, the majority of the committee felt that it would be wise to avoid a close association with any leftist groups. Years later, during the damaging McCarthy and McCarran investigations, Price and others were glad that the group had maintained this policy.

The committee cooperated with a host of other organizations which were concentrating upon peace, aid to China,

or the development of a more internationalist foreign policy.
Prominent within the last category of organizations was
William Allen White's Committee to Defend America by Aiding
the Allies, founded in May 1940. Included in its program
was a clause calling for the withholding of war materials
from aggressor nations.[24] The efforts of this committee
proved to be a factor permitting the eventual termination
of efforts by the American Committee for Non-Participation
in Japanese Aggression.

In addition to these national organizations, the
committee cooperated with many local groups, including
over eighty affiliated local committees. These local
committees sprang up largely during 1939 in cities such as
Boston, Baltimore, Richmond, Durham, Pittsburg, Cleveland,
Toledo, Chicago, Kansas City, Minneapolis, Denver, Seattle,
Portland, San Francisco and Los Angeles. Some were stimulated,
but not directly organized, by the national committee. It
became the policy of the national organization to regard them
in all cases as autonomous, and to try only to offer them
support and information rather than to control their activities.

Literally hundreds of local groups cooperated with
the committee as well as these affiliated local organizations.
These included church groups, business associations, civic
and professional clubs, labor unions, women's organizations,
foreign policy study groups and the like. The committee
provided these local organizations with information and encouraged them to register in Washington their support of an
end to the export of war supplies to Japan.

The possibility of cooperating with organizations
in other countries which were working to halt the shipment
of essential war materials to Japan was mentioned in *America's*

Share in Japan's War Guilt .[25] However, very little was actually
done along these lines, primarily because the committee lacked
the requisite funds, time and contacts.

No aspect of the committee's work was more basic than
the preparation and wide distribution of information and
literature. In addition to its initial booklet, *America's
Share in Japan's War Guilt,* it prepared two more pamphlets,
a succession of leaflets and fliers, and special lists of
qualified speakers and writers on the Far East. To its own
members it sent out a succession of over forty memoranda, each
containing fresh information and suggestions for action. There
were also many special mailings, the largest of which was sent
to over a hundred thousand Protestant pastors throughout
America, asking them to ponder the question of American military
aid to Japan.

As the committee recognized, the two greatest channels
of public information on current issues at that time were
the press and the radio. It sent out well over fifty factual
newspaper releases to the press dealing with the work of the
committee, results of public opinion polls, trade statistics
and other news relating to America and the Far East. Beyond
these official releases, several members--notably Greene,
Price and Mrs. Fitch--wrote numerous letters to the editors
of many leading newspapers, sometimes objecting to specific
articles or editorials. As its efforts became better known,
newspapers grew to be increasingly receptive to the releases
of the committee as useful sources of information and opinion.
On a more personal basis the organization also arranged a
series of interviews and luncheons with leading editors,
publishers and columnists.

The committee also sought to present its views over

the radio. Network **broadcasts** were arranged for Stimson, Judd, Greene, Price, Yarnell, Carlson and others, and well over a hundred talks with various members were **presented** over local broadcasts. Through the supply of factual information and personal interviews, the group offered to provide relevant information to radio commentators.

In September 1938 the committee set up a Speakers' Bureau in its New York headquarters under the general supervision of Mrs. Price. The bureau soon found it impossible to handle the complexities of such an operation, and it evolved into an **informal** clearinghouse for speakers. Among those who conducted extensive speaking tours under committee auspices were Dr. Walter Judd, Mrs. George Fitch, Major Evans Carlson and Miss Freda Utley. Dr. Judd **himself** gave over 1400 talks during the period in which the committee was operating;[26] reportedly, members of Congress could trace his trips across the states by mail appeals demanding passage of embargo legislation.[27]

Finally, though the committee relied much more on personal contacts, direct mailings and group meetings than on magazine articles, several members had articles dealing with issues relating to American non-participation in Japanese aggression published in periodicals.

For the two and a half years of its existence, thus, the committee, though composed of a small group of busy people, managed to employ to some extent every channel of communication available to it. In terms of the range of its publicity and information efforts, it was certainly the most active non-government organization dealing with the Far Eastern situation, and perhaps, with America's role in international affairs in general--at least until the emergence of the Committee to

Defend America by Aiding the Allies and the America First
Committee in the middle of 1940.

In order to finance its extensive campaign, the committee required a constant flow of funds. As is evident from
even the most casual reading of its records, this problem of
finances was an unceasing burden; in addition to periodic
appeals to known supporters and new groups, the officers were
forced to include a plea for contributions in much of their
correspondence. For the two and a half years of its active
campaign, the committee received almost $140,000 for its
expenses. Nearly all of this income--more than 95 per cent of it--
came from the more than 8000 contributions which it received.[28]
Although itemizations of specific contributions and detailed
financial records are no longer available, a study of the
correspondence reveals that a relatively small number of
active members made frequent and substantial donations, and
that these were supplemented to an extensive degree by a large
number of smaller gifts. The larger contributions generally
came from wealthy people who had strong international interests
and strong feelings about China.[29] The remainder of the organization's funds were obtained from the sale of literature--
mainly to supporting groups--and from a very small net income
from its Speakers' Bureau.[30]

Chapter III

POLICY

Unlike many other groups of its kind--at least many
of its contemporaries--the American Committee for Non-Participation in Japanese Aggression confined itself to its original,
precisely defined purpose. In its first official statement,
the booklet *America's Share in Japan's War Guilt*, the committee
sharply limited its objectives:

> The central and single aim of the Committee is expressed
> in the phrase "non-participation in Japanese aggression."
> Doctrinal isms, domestic issues, and the European situation,
> however important, are beyond its scope.[1]

Under the shrewd guidance of Harry Price, it studiously avoided
expanding its efforts into significant yet extraneous causes.
As Dr. Walter Judd recalls:

> The Committee had no other important goals than the
> main one indicated in the Committee's name, to stop the
> vital assistance the United States, or people and firms,
> were giving to the Japanese military's ruthless aggression
> in China....[2]

There were several practical reasons for the committee's
concentration upon this single objective. First, it was the
one issue on which all members of the group were fully united;
the wide range of political views represented by its members
would have made agreement on any broader issues unlikely.
Second, the majority felt that if they concentrated upon the
single objective of stopping American economic support to

Japan's military effort, there would be less likelihood of
dissipating their energies and failing to attain their goal.
Third, many members--notably Price himself--felt that a concentration upon the clear, practical, specific goal of stopping
American aid to Japan's military machine would be more likely
than a diffuse program to challenge isolationist attitudes and,
perhaps, to help furnish an effective precedent for a more
responsible American role in international affairs.[3] Although
members of the committee willingly conceded that many other
goals were naturally and logically related to the group's
efforts, most felt that these other aims should not divert
the organization too far from its central purpose. This
selective approach was facilitated by the existence of other
groups concerned with a wider range of foreign policy objectives.

Although the impetus of the committee's campaign for non-
participation was directed mainly toward the realization of an
embargo upon the export of war supplies to Japan, a second
closely related means of reducing American economic support
to Japanese aggression always lurked not far in the background--
restrictions upon imports from Japan. In a preliminary report
of the technical committee, the conclusion was reached that
"American purchases from Japan are as great a means of
assistance to Japan, if not greater, as American sale of
war materials to her." Because of this fact, the technical
committee recommended that the committee avoid speaking solely
of the embargo and instead use some phrase that would refer to
import restrictions as well.[4] The group was willing to accept
this broader conception of its slogan "non-participation in
Japanese aggression," but for the reasons discussed in the
first chapter, it continued to concentrate primarily upon
the embargo.

During the campaign, references to import restrictions became more pronounced in the committee's literature and correspondence. Even its first booklet mentioned as a goal "the stoppage of war credits and essential war supplies to Japan...."[5] After recommendations from members including Maxwell Stewart[6] and Roger Greene,[7] the National Board decided on January 3, **1940,** to put "increasing emphasis upon import restrictions by Administrative action."[8] By March the national headquarters was advising its affiliated local committees to express support to the Administration for "tariff restrictions upon imports from Japan which make possible her continuing purchase of war supplies abroad."[9] In spite of this growing emphasis, however, the embargo upon American war materials to Japan remained the most spectacular aspect of the committee's program, the aspect its members now remember best.

Several other goals were naturally connected to the goal of American non-participation in Japanese aggression; and though the committee made some attempt to avoid dealing with these issues, it found that almost by accident they crept into its program. Most prominent among these related objectives was support of nonmilitary, humanitarian aid for China.

In *America's Share in Japan's War Guilt* the committee itself never spoke of supplying such aid to China, but one of the authorities whom it quoted raised the possibility of even military aid to China; "If we want to sell war materials, let us sell them in wholesale lots to China so she may be more able to defend herself against her barbaric enemy...."[10] On August 29, 1939, in an official information release, the committee recommended that its members give "useful support" to several possible policies, including "further aid to China, e.g., a credit for currency stabilization or for industrial development."[11] In another statement released on September 14, 1939, it indicated the logic by which a policy of aid to China could evolve out of one of non-participation in Japanese aggression:

> The firm withholding of such support through the proposed embargo on war materials to Japan and perhaps through restrictions upon imports from Japan would lead even more quickly now to the bogging down of Japan's military machine and to the emergence of an independent China as a guarantee for our own security as well as for future peace in Asia. This outcome would be further ensured through peaceful aid to China for relief and economic reconstruction.[12]

Committee members recall no dispute within the organization over the issue of such aid to China, primarily because nearly all of the active members were friends of China and sympathetic with the Chinese people. But, were there not some members and supporters who felt that American aid to China would constitute participation in the Sino-Japanese conflict of the very sort that they believed the United States must avoid? Indeed, there were such people, though they remained a very small minority. Representative of this cautious group was one of the honorary vice-chairmen, Dr. A. Lawrence Lowell. When asked for his approval of several measures including the support of financial aid and relief assistance for China,[13] Dr. Lowell replied charily:

> While I heartily approve of forbidding the export of scrap iron & petroleum to Japan, the letter includes other matters outside of the scope of our Non-Participation Committee, on which I am not prepared to express an opinion, without further consideration.[14]

Without a doubt, members like Dr. Lowell were a strong factor
in keeping the committee's efforts centrally directed upon
the original non-participation program.

How did the committee propose to realize its objective
of non-participation in Japanese aggression? As Edgar H. Rue
explained to a potential supporter:

> We are working to effect three ends: (first) to create
> a public opinion against our participation in Japan's
> ruthless, unjustifiable invasion of China, (second) to
> bring this public opinion to bear upon our Chief Executive
> for executive action and upon Secretary Hull and the
> Department of State to change our foreign policy, (three)
> to bring pressure upon Congress for legislative action.[15]

The spread of information and interest among the general public
has been discussed in the previous chapter, but on what basis
did the committee propose to convert this public opinion into
government action to withhold our support from Japan's
military efforts? In light of its goals, this question re-
solves itself into a more specific one: On what basis did
the committee propose that the United States embargo the export
of war supplies to Japan?

First, it dismissed the Neutrality Act of 1937 as an
inadequate basis for an embargo. Since the act referred only to
munitions, Japan still could obtain from the United States
the raw materials and machinery which were vastly more
important to her than munitions; unlike China, Japan had a
highly developed munitions industry and a large merchant
marine for transporting these supplies from America to
Japan.[16] Moreover, the revised Neutrality Act of 1939,
it was felt, was framed with a view primarily to the European

conflict and would not be suitable for application to the
Far Eastern situation.[17]

  After discussing other possible bases for an embargo,
the group decided to focus upon Japan's violation of a solemn
peace treaty to which both Japan and the United States were
signatories--the Nine-Power Treaty of 1922. Within the context of violations of this treaty, there were two possible
approaches, each reflected in a separate bill introduced in
Congress in the spring of 1939.

  The first approach provided for the protection and
preservation of rights guaranteed to the United States under
provisions of the Nine-Power Treaty. In this treaty all
signatories agreed to maintain the Open Door principle of
equal opportunity for all nations in their trade with China.
Japan not only had violated the treaty by forcibly disrupting
our China trade through the imposition of illegal restrictions
upon it, but had also confiscated American property and endangered American lives. The committee argued that the
United States would be perfectly justified under international
law in prohibiting the export of supplies that were being
used in the violation of her own treaty rights.[18]

  This first approach was taken in a bill introduced
by Senator Key Pittman. Written with some assistance from
members of the committee, this bill would authorize the President to place restrictions upon trade--both imports and exports
(except agricultural products)--and credits between the United
States and any nation which, through violation of the Nine-
Power Pact, endangered the lives of American citizens or
deprived them of their legal rights and privileges under the
terms of that treaty.

  The second, more extensively employed approach was

based upon the United States' obligations under the Nine-
Power Treaty. The first article of the treaty required all
contracting powers other than China to respect the sovereignty,
the independence, and the territorial and administrative
integrity of China. America's support to Japan's invasion of
China was clearly inconsistent with these obligations; for
instead of helping to preserve China's independence, the United
States was aiding and abetting in its violation. The United
States, the committee strongly maintained, was obligated by
the treaty to terminate the export of war supplies being used
to violate the sovereignty, the independence, and the territorial and administrative integrity of a nation whose sovereignty
and integrity the United States was pledged to respect.

A bill introduced in the Senate by Senator Lewis B.
Schwellenbach and in the House by Representative Monrad C.
Wallgren employed this second approach. Also written with
some cooperation from members of the committee, this bill
would authorize the President to withhold from export all
materials (except agricultural products) which there was
reason to believe would be used to violate the sovereignty
and integrity of a nation whose sovereignty and integrity
the United States was obligated by treaty to respect.

For more than a year following the introduction of
these bills in the spring of 1939, the committee pressed
for a passage of one or another of them. In its official
releases, in its correspondence, in appearances before
Congressional committees, in interviews with government
leaders--in all of its efforts, the committee concentrated
upon securing an embargo on the export of war materials to
Japan on the basis of her violations of the Nine-Power Treaty.

However, with the German invasion of the Low Countries

on May 10, 1940, the group's strategy underwent a significant
shift; the committee then recommended that Congress pass
export restrictions not on the basis of treaty violations
by Japan but on the basis of the need for conserving national
resources needed for America's own defense.

The chronology of the events surrounding this shift
is important enough to relate in some detail. On the morning
of Friday, May 10, when Americans learned of the German
invasion of Holland and Belgium, Roger Greene called Harry
Price, who was then in Washington, and recommended that he
speak immediately to Senator Pittman, proposing the idea
of basing export restrictions upon the necessity of conserving America's national resources. This suggestion was
well received by Pittman. Since it was known that relations
between Pittman and Secretary Hull were then severely strained
because of a dispute over the trade agreements legislation,
Price asked Senator Pittman if he would have any objection
to mentioning his opinion in this matter to people in the
State Department. Pittman was quite willing, and Price went
immediately to see Stanley Hornbeck, chief advisor on Far
Eastern affairs in the Department of State, who said that
he would relay the information without delay to Secretary Hull.
On the following Sunday, May 12, the Secretary and Senator
Pittman held a long conference in Mr. Hull's home where they
discussed such action.[19]

The next Friday, May 17, Greene wrote to Secretary
Hull, indicating that the committee was prepared to urge
strong public support for a general law authorizing the
President to withhold from export basic war materials for
the purpose of conserving our national resources and pro-
tecting our national security. Of course, wrote Greene, the
law would have a suitable provision for exemption in the case

when exported articles were to be used in a manner compatible
with America's national interest.[20]

The result of all these efforts was the incorporation--
into a bill already in preparation that dealt with the en-
largement of America's entire military establishment--of a
section authorizing the President to withdraw from export
supplies and equipment deemed essential for the national
defense. This National Defense Bill passed the House on May
24 and the Senate on June 11 and was signed into law by the
President on July 2, 1940. On the same day he issued the first
of a series of proclamations requiring that licenses be
secured for the export of a whole range of war materials
crucial to Japan.

Greene's recommendation of May 10 that the embargo
be based upon the needs of national defense had been discussed
by the committee on several previous occasions, but had always
been rejected in favor of an approach based on violations of
the Nine-Power Treaty. On November 8, 1939, Pearl Buck had
written to Price that instead of an active, open embargo, the
United States could find less dangerous ways of reaching the
same end:

> The United States government can find for instance
> that it needs its own scrap iron and must keep its own
> supplies of gas and oils and that its ammunition making
> factories required their services for other kinds of
> orders.[21]

Price, however, maintained that many articles and supplies
crucial to Japan's war-making capacity could not be reached
through this type of approach.[22]

After speaking with Secretary Hull on April 18, 1940,
though, Price became more receptive to export restrictions

of this type, noting that the State Department would welcome
a discretionary law authorizing such restrictions if it could
be reasonably sure of the law's passage without the raising
of a political storm.[23]   As Greene pointed out in his letter
of May 17, 1940, to Hull, an embargo based upon national
security would be unlikely to raise the type of storm featured
by Hull since it would be very difficult to oppose.[24]   Also,
as the European conflict loomed increasingly large in the
minds of Americans, the committee found it correspondingly
more difficult to concentrate the attention of Congress upon
an embargo aimed exclusively at Japan.[25]   It realized that
export controls based upon the needs of national defense
would stand a greater chance of passage.   Thus, by the time
of the German invasion of the Low Countries, the Committee
had discussed an embargo based upon national security as a
possible alternative to one based upon Japanese violation of
the Nine-Power Treaty.

The actual role of the committee in the development
of the relevant section of the National Defense Act is extremely difficult to assess. As Greene himself replied to
an inquiry:

> When great natural forces and events are at work, it
> is difficult to guess how much one's own efforts have
> contributed to results like these, especially since our
> officials are hesitant about telling the processes by
> which ends were accomplished.[26]

But the chronology of events leading up to the final passage
of the bill certainly suggests that the efforts of the
committee played a part. Also, the President's proclamation
of articles to be controlled followed another intensive effort
by the group.

In *The Road to Pearl Harbor* Herbert Feis claims that
the embargo section was added at the urging of the army.[27]
But in light of the committee's activities, including a short
letter written on May 21, 1940, by Greene to Major General C.
M. Wesson, **urging** the support of the army for an embargo of
aid to Japan's military machine, Feis' interpretation is open
to serious question.[28] The catalyst behind the inclusion of
the embargo section into the National Defense Bill may not have
been the army, as Feis indicates, but the committee.

In order to mobilize public and Congressional opinion
behind an embargo on the export of American war supplies to
Japan, the committee had to establish the positive advantages
of such a policy. In its appeals to the American public, it
strove to de-emphasize the more emotional justifications for
an embargo, concentrating instead upon the tangible, real
advantages which would accrue to the United States.

First and foremost, the committee argued that the
present policy of supporting Japan was endangering the ultimate
safety of the United States, and that on the basis of its
national security the United States must cease exporting crucial
military materials to Japan. In claiming that Japanese expansion
threatened vital American interests, it first had to define,
if only by implication, what America's vital interests in the
Far East were. Having located these interests, it then could
show how Japanese expansion was threatening them.

China always occupied a central position in any of
the committee's definitions of the requirements of American
security: the maintenance of a strong, independent China was
seen as a critical, stabilizing force in the Far East. The
group argued that a strong China would prevent Japanese or

Russian domination of Asia, **either of which would seriously**
disrupt the traditional balance of power in Asia.[29] Committee
literature and correspondence often spoke of the emergence of
a healthy, democratic China as "the surest guarantee of future
peace and cooperation in the Pacific."[30] In Stimson's letter
of January 11, 1940, to the *New York Times*, he stressed that
the history of America's involvement in the Far East represented the conviction that the "continuance of the stability and
independence of the naturally peaceful culture of the Chinese
nation" was among "the far sighted interests of our own
country."[31]

    Gradually, the committee's conception of the role of
China expanded to make China a stabilizing force not merely
in the Far East but in the entire world as well. In its booklet published in April 1940, *Shall America Stop Arming Japan?*
the committee warned that only "with an independent and
developing China can there be maintained peace and security
in Asia, and security for all nations that border the
Pacific."[32] The committee explicitly associated the maintenance of stability in the Western hemisphere with the
continued independence of China.[33] After the German attack
on Holland, Belgium, and France in May and June 1940, the
group's literature came to link Great Britain and China
together as the two last allies of the United States:

> The ABC of this matter is that *America* now has but
> two certain allies left, *Britain* and *China*, for the task
> of preserving and rebuilding liberty, democracy, security,
> and cooperation in the world.[34]

    Although the most vital American interest endangered
by Japan was an independent China, there were several other
interests that would be placed in jeopardy by continued

Japanese expansion. The most important of these were the
Philippine Islands and the Dutch East Indies. The Philippines,
as a possession of the United States, were entitled to American
defense until they would be granted their independence in 1946.
The United States was importing critical raw materials from
the Philippines as well as from the Dutch East Indies. As
itemized in an address by Admiral Yarnell early in 1940, the
United States received 850,000 tons per year of sugar from
the Philippines, practically all of its rubber from the Dutch
East Indies, Malaya and Indo-China, most of its tin from the
South China Sea area, all of its quinine from the Dutch East
Indies, and all of its chromite from the Philippines. "Of
our seven major imports," Yarnell concluded, "six are major
exports from the Far East."[35]

Beyond this region, the committee noted, vital American
interests were threatened all the way back across the Pacific.
It argued that Japanese expansion, if unchecked, could increasingly become a menace to America on issues of crucial
importance: "The United States would face increasing problems
in connection with South America, North Pacific fisheries,
Hawaii and Panama defenses, and our own markets."[36]

In addition to this danger which Japanese expansion,
supported by our exports, represented to American interests,
our exports to Japan weakened American security by seriously
depleting our essential national resources. This aspect of
the problem did not receive primary emphasis in the committee's
literature and correspondence until May 1940 when, as has
been described, it proposed the retention of national resources as the basis for an embargo of exports of war materials
to Japan. Nevertheless, as early as May 1939, after a meeting
with a group from the Iron and Steel Independent Producers

Committee on Scrap, Price cooperated with these men in pub-
licizing the shortages of scrap iron and scrap steel due to
their large export, especially to Japan.[37] In some of its
later literature, such as the leaflet *America Supports
Japanese Aggression,* the committee began to treat this
aspect of the problem: "...we are seriously depleting some
of our own resources, essential for defense--notably scrap
iron and high-grade gasolene and oil."[38] In a press release
dated February 13, 1940, it linked America's demand for scrap
iron to the need for export restrictions: "The depletion
of domestic supplies, causing shortages and rising prices for
manufacturers of steel, furnishes further reason for such
restrictions at this time."[39] Thus, not only would the export
of war materials to Japan help to build up a Japanese military
machine that would become a growing threat to America's vital
interests, but also this export would have a deleterious effect
upon the strengthening of America's own military establishment.

The second basis on which the committee recommended an
embargo upon our trade with Japan was America's economic self-
interest. This argument had two aspects: the potential loss
of trade in the Far East, and the increased defense expenditures
required at home.

The first aspect centered around the loss of American
trade with China if Japan were able to consolidate her victories
in the Far East. As the committee noted in its first booklet:
"It is clear, propaganda to the contrary notwithstanding, that
an independent China will trade with the world, while a con-
quered China will trade almost exclusively with Japan."[40]
Since American trade with China had never been large--not nearly
as large as her trade with Japan--it usually spoke about the
loss of future trade, about China as "the world's greatest

potential market."[41] It emphasized especially the tremendous potentialities of trade with a free post-war China:

> Thousands of miles of railway lines, tens of thousands
> of miles in new roads, tens or hundreds of thousands of
> automobiles, vessels for a coast-wise merchant marine,
> expansion of national airways and of communication systems,
> and the reestablishment of industries destroyed by the
> war and their extension throughout the interior provinces--
> all these are within the scope of probability once
> reconstruction in an independent, peaceful and unified
> China gets under way.[42]

This tendency to think of Chinese trade in terms of some 400,000,000 prospective customers permeated the committee's thinking just as it had permeated the thinking of American businessmen about the Chinese market for well over a century.

To those who claimed that it was foolish to antagonize Japan, America's best customer in the Far East, the committee answered that the immediate profits from America's war-time trade with Japan were more than offset by the losses in her peace-time trade with Japan in such commodities as raw cotton, lumber, kerosene and paper.[43] With regard to cotton, it published a special booklet *The Far Eastern Conflict and American Cotton*, which indicated how American cotton exports to Japan had been drastically cut as a result of Japan's prohibition of the manufacture of cotton textiles for domestic use, except for military purposes. The American cotton industry, the committee cautioned, could expect only continued decline in its exports to Japan as long as the war continued.[44]

The committee also identified Japan's labor system particularly in occupied China, as a future threat to "the

peace, security and economic structure of the world for years
to come." In what seems now to be a crudely stated view of
international economics, it claimed:

> ...we are helping also to set up a competitor that, through
> expropriation of resources and utilization of almost un-
> limited subsistence labor, may in time produce a mount-
> ing tide of cheap manufactures with which American industry,
> at American wage levels, could scarcely compete.[45]

But not only was American trade with Japan dangerously
threatening the economic interests of the United States, it
also was requiring the United States to spend more and more
money upon defense: "The irony of it! We prepare to defend
ourselves against those whose sinews of strength for expansion
come from our own industries."[46] Thus, the immediate profits
from America's war-time trade with Japan were far overshadowed
by the long-term losses in peace-time trade and the enormous
increases in America's defense expenditures.

The third basis on which the committee advocated an
embargo involved its view of America's proper contribution
toward the restoration of international law and order, an
international law and order which Japan was so violently
upsetting. The committee felt that a Japanese victory in
China would encourage and strengthen the hands of aggressive
powers elsewhere. Instead of being discredited, aggression
as an instrument of national policy would be further established.
In September 1940 Harry Price in his widely distributed essay
"Pacific Strategy" linked American self-interest to the maintenance of peace throughout the world:

> Ultimate American security and prosperity can be
> assured only when there has been a defeat and a

discrediting of ruthless arbitrary forces in international
relations, and when relations among those nations of the
world that desire justice, law and order achieve **sufficient**
strength and unity to discourage further aggression.[47]

However, this highly non-isolationist interpretation
of the requirements of American security was not accompanied
by a correspondingly comprehensive formulation of the role
that America must play in international affairs. In the same
article in which Price outlined the basic conditions of
American security in such broad terms, he also enumerated the
four points of an American strategy with which to attain
these ends: increased aid to China, an understanding with
Russia, a closer accord with the Pacific Islands, and the
cutting-off of aid to Japan.[48]   But nowhere in this article
did Price, certainly one of the most perceptive and progressive members of the committee, acknowledge the necessity
for actual American defense commitments in the Far East.   In
all fairness to Price, though, it must be pointed out that
in the peculiar climate of prewar America, few people saw
any contradiction between a belief, on the one hand, that
America had to play an important role in world **affairs** and
a belief, on the other hand, that this objective could be
effectively pursued by means other than extensive military
commitments.

Like many Americans, most members of the committee
apparently thought that America could make her presence felt
on the international scene through means more idealistic, less
sordid than military intervention. A refusal to assist Japan
in her invasion of China "would help to restore the prestige
and sanctity of international obligations."[49] More positively,
the United States could "inject into international relations

in this area a new and broadened perspective based upon equality
and mutual advantage for all nations."[50] If the methods of
the committee now seem naive in this age of armed intervention
in Vietnam and the Dominican Republic, its recognition of
America's vital interest in the maintenance of law and order,
even in the more remote regions of the world, was far ahead
of the prevailing isolationist temper of its milieu.

The fourth basis on which the committee defended an
embargo was America's historic friendship with China. In all its
efforts, it sought to emphasize the concrete significance of
China for America; it constantly strove to de-emphasize any senti-
mental attachment to China. As has been discussed, the committee
stressed the importance to American security of the maintenance
of a strong, independent China and the importance to American
trade of free access to the markets of the Far East. It also
spoke of more than a century of American involvement in China,
of a series of American trade agreements with China stretching
back to 1842, of John Hay's Open Door notes, of America's reply
to Japan's Twenty-One Demands of 1915 and her subsequent defense of China's rights at the Versailles Conference, of the
Nine-Power Treaty of 1922, and of Stimson's "non-recognition"
note of 1932. America's historical friendship with China,
the committee concluded, was based on the recognition that a
policy of justice and amity for China was to the best advantage of the United States.[51]

Amity for China, however, was never foremost in the
committee's itemization of the positive reasons for embargoing the export of war supplies to Japan. From the very beginning of its campaign, it realized that if it should stress
primarily the point of friendship for China, it might well
be thought of simply as a pro-China pressure group. For this

same reason, whenever possible, it refused direct contributions from Chinese citizens and eschewed close contacts with any other organizations dominated by Chinese.[52] As its leaders recognized, the committee would never be successful unless it could present its non-participation program as an American policy solidly based on American self-interest.

The fifth and final basis for an embargo was the belief, almost universal both inside and outside of the Committee, that trade with Japan in war materials was immoral. *America's Share in Japan's War Guilt* pointed to the injustice of American policy: "We are committing a great wrong. We are virtual allies of a nation whose military policy and methods have received world condemnation."[53] Although the committee throughout its campaign sought to rely chiefly upon rational persuasion rather than upon highly charged emotional appeals, those who cooperated with the organization out of moral indignation were perhaps its most enthusiastic and loyal supporters.

Chapter IV

OPPOSITION .

In its two-and-a-half-year campaign, the committee
constantly dealt with a series of objections from the general
public to its recommended policy of non-participation in
Japanese aggression and especially to the proposed embargo
on the export of war supplies to Japan. First and foremost
among these objections was the fear that an embargo would
lead to war with Japan.

In the National Board meetings of the committee were
frequently aired such statements as that of Dr. Judd:
"There is a great deal more wariness in regard to our side
of the case....People think they are going to be swept
into war."[1] Even if people could not establish by just
what process an embargo would lead America into war with
Japan, many still felt, like Kenneth Scott Latourette, the
distinguished historian of Christianity and the Far East,
that "an embargo in itself is a warlike act."[2] Public
sentiment against war was so strong that the committee's
efforts occasionally resolved themselves into arguing why
war was not likely to result from the imposition of an
embargo.

First, the committee claimed: "There is no historical support for the supposition that an American embargo
on war materials to Japan would lead to war."[3] Not only
were critics of the committee unable to find any historical
illustration of an embargo which resulted in war, but Henry
Douglas, a researcher for the group, published a short article

which **recounted** the successful results which accrued from
the American embargo of 1918 against Japan.[4]

In addition to this **historical precedent**, the committee could point to contemporary ones: "France, Russia,
and even New Zealand and French **Indo-China**, **have had restrictions**
upon their war commerce with Japan; in no case did this lead
to conflict."[5] In a letter to Senator Schwellenbach, Roger
Greene wrote that though there had been a **traditional** enmity
between Russia and Japan, though Russia had provoked Japan
far **more** than had the United States, though war with Russia--
unlike war with the United States--would not cripple Japanese
trade, though Russia was considerably more vulnerable than
the United States, and though Russia was currently occupied
in her war with Finland, Japan still had not attacked Russia.
For many of the same reasons that governed her restraint
with Russia, Greene concluded, it would be very improbable
that Japan would attack the United States.[6]

The fundamental argument used by the committee to
minimize the possibility of war with Japan resulting from
America's imposition of an embargo was simply the futility,
even the impertinence, of weak Japan attacking powerful America:
"Is it likely that Japan, extended and belabored during two
years of exhausting warfare, would endeavor to 'take on'
the world's strongest industrial nation simply because we
chose to stop selling her our own war materials?"[7] As
itemized in a memorandum by T.A. Bisson, Japan's coal shortage,
power famine, shutdown of major industries, scarcity of
consumer goods, exhaustion of gold reserves, difficulties
over rice supplies, and insufficiency of man power would make
war with the United States "foolhardy in the extreme."[8] In
retrospect, it is evident that the committee, like most

government **leaders, grossly** overestimated the deterioration
of Japan's economic condition as a result of the **Sino-Japanese**
War; in this prewar period few people thought in Keynesian
terms of the **beneficent** effect of a war upon a nation's
economy.

Another factor mitigating against a Japanese war **with**
the United States was the resultant loss **to Japan** of her
trade with the United States. War would stop the sale of
many American goods, crucial to Japan, but not included in
any **proposed** embargo.[9] And not only would Japan be **deprived**
of access to the **markets of the** United States, but also she
would have great difficulty in getting resources **from other**
countries as well, since Europe would be keeping its resources
at home, and the United States could easily stop Japanese
commerce with Latin America.[10]

But, many people argued, war might come about by
means other than by the Japanese undertaking systematic
military and naval operations against the United **States.**
Might not Japan provoke the American government and people
into war through a series of incidents? In a personal letter
to the Ambassador to **Japan,**Joseph C. Grew, Greene squarely
met these doubts. He conceded that America could **expect** an
increase in the number and severity of such incidents, but
argued that there was not very much more **that Japan** could
do in China against American **interests that she** had not already
done. Greene concluded: "The American government and people
are sufficiently wise and patient to avoid being drawn into
war unnecessarily merely because of additional Japanese
provocation of the kind that we have observed hitherto."[11]
Interestingly, **Greene, in a later** letter to Senator Schwellenbach,
pointed to America's "restraint" at the time of the Panay

incident; many others had called America's reaction to this episode not restraint but cowardice.[12]

If Japan could not provoke America into war by provoking her in China, might she not respond to an embargo by sending an expedition to the Philippines or to the Dutch East Indies? For many of the same reasons that would inhibit Japan from attacking Russia or the United States, the committee replied, she would be very unlikely to move against the Philippines or the Dutch East Indies. Roger Greene felt that, involved as she was in China, Japan could not afford to divert even a few divisions from China or Japan to attempt such a venture; and her transportation network, overburdened by the task of provisioning her army in China, would be grossly inadequate for supplying an army as distant as the Philippines or the Dutch East Indies.[13] Also, Greene reported that the Dutch were prepared to blow up their wells in the event of a Japanese invasion; thus, Japan probably would get less oil from there than she would if she made no attack.[14] With regard to the Philippines, the committee pointed out that an attack there would result in the loss for Japan of important markets both there and in the United States as well as in Europe and South America; the United States could certainly block the latter from Japanese trade.[15] The American campaign for the suppression of the Philippine insurrection, Greene argued, provided an example to the Japanese of the tremendous difficulties involved in such a venture in that region.[16] Thus, just as the committee had dismissed the possibility of war with Japan resulting from a direct attack upon the United States or from a series of provocations, so also did it discount the chance of war resulting from a Japanese invasion of the Philippines or the Dutch East Indies.

In retrospect, it is apparent that the committee tended to underestimate the possibility of war. Certainly, some of its members resorted to exaggerated statements concerning the improbability of war. Before the Senate Committee on Foreign Relations on April 25, 1939, Dr. Judd testified that the enactment of embargo legislation "will have minimum cost, and almost no risk to ourselves...."[17] Or, on March 11, 1940, in a letter to Latourette, Greene announced in no uncertain terms: "So far as I can remember, no person with real experience in the Far East during the last 10 years has any fear that an embargo would lead to war."[18]

From about the spring of 1940 onward, however, there was a definite evolution in the attitude of many of the committee members, which was reflected in the correspondence, literature, and bulletins. There was a diminution of much of the wishful thinking that had been present in the earlier days of the committee and an increasing awareness of the possibility of war. Particularly evident were a growing consciousness of the real risks in either policy--continuing to support Japanese aggression or not continuing--and a recognition that both sets of risks must be faced. In *Shall America Stop Arming Japan?* printed in April 1940, the committee emphasized the dangers inherent in either course of action:

> Firmness, courage, and ·a sense of justice in determining our own conduct may prove far less hazardous in the end than a frightened policy of immediate expediency. Those who insist, rightly, that the possible consequences of any action should be weighed, should face also the necessity of weighing the far

more serious consequences that may result from inaction--
from lack of the moral stamina required to remove ourselves
from the role of "Japan's partner."[19]

In addition to this fear of war, the committee was
confronted with a spate of other public objections to an
embargo against Japan. There was, for example, a feeling
among the American people that even if the United States
were to take a firm stand against Japan's aggression in
China, Great Britain and France would be very likely to
yield to Japanese pressure and to "sell out" China. To
allay this fear, the committee argued: "The British and the
French, with public opinion opposed to Japan, with their
strong desire to retain American good will, and with their
own Far Eastern interests at stake, would not be likely to
adopt measures in opposition to such an affirmative American
policy."[20]

A more prominent objection concerned the effectiveness
of a one-power embargo: In the event of an American embargo,
would Japan merely shift her trade from us to other powers?
In a report of the technical committee on June 20, 1938,
Professor Eugene Staley was quoted: "The result of a single-
handed withholding of supplies would be a diversion of trade
away from the United States without effectively handicapping
Japan."[21] However, the committee did not share this view;
it believed that a unilateral embargo would severely hamper
Japan's military effort. Some essential materials, such as
machinery and machine tools, special steels and lubricating
oils, it claimed, could be obtained only from the United
States; and others, especially scrap iron, could not be
gotten in sufficient quantities elsewhere. Germany and Italy
could not supply Japan with what she needed even if they

wanted to do so; purchases from Russia and France were
already checked; and in Great Britain public opinion would
prohibit any government policy in the Far East which appeared
to run counter to that of the United States.[22] Most of
the objections to the effectiveness of a unilateral embargo
by the United States disappeared with the beginning of the
European War on September 3, 1939; after that date nearly
all acknowledged that it would be virtually impossible for
Japan to get any of her war supplies from Europe.

Related to the problem of a possible transfer of
Japanese trade from the United States to other countries
was the complicated problem of enforcement of American trade
restrictions. Specifically, how was the United States
to prevent American producers from selling to nations favor-
able or at least indifferent to Japan, who would then resell
the same goods to Japan?[23] The negligible amount of discussion
concerning this problem suggests that the committee leadership
felt that it was, at the moment, more hypothetical than actual
and need not be dealt with at length unless it proved to be
a real problem.

Another, more common public objection to the proposed
embargo stemmed from the pacifist neutralist doctrine that to
avoid war the United States must treat all nations exactly
the same. The committee immediately set out to demolish the
assumptions on which such a view of the role of America in
international affairs was based. In its first booklet the Reverend
E.W. Luccock was quoted as asserting that America's peace
efforts based on this neutralist philosophy "have been ineffective because they have been in terms of cynicism,
cowardice and irresponsibility, instead of terms of ex-
pectation, courage and honorable action."[24] With respect

to Quaker pacifists, Greene observed: "it never appeared to me that the Quaker position involved helping a criminal for reasons of profit or fear."[25] The committee argued that in relation to Japan's aggression, pacifist neutrality was neither moral nor possible. The United States had to take a position in the Sino-Japanese War since if it "did nothing," its resources would continue to aid Japan; and if that aid were withdrawn, it would be helping China. Since a decision had to be made, the committee concluded, the United States should make the one most consistent with its own self-interest and with justice--to cease to aid Japan in its ruthless aggression in China.[26] Although some of its supporters were sympathetic to the doctrines of pacifism, Price probably represented the sentiment of a substantial majority when he wrote: "Pacifism, rooted in the abhorrence of war, has blinded many...to the worse evil of human subjugation to tyranny, and to rule by force alone."[27]

In the course of its campaign, the committee found that pacifist neutrality as a doctrine tended to falter when applied specifically to the issue of American military support to Japan. As has been noted, the United States simply could not be neutral in the Far East; and once "neutralists" acknowledged this fact, they often swung over to a position similar to that of the committee, though at times with residual misgivings. A committee survey of editorial opinion estimated that about twenty-five per cent of the big-money metropolitan newspapers underwent a change of this sort. Forced to choose between their shibboleths of "war-meddling" and "keep-hands-off," on the one hand, and their desire to stop American support of Japan's brutality in China, on the other hand, most of these newspapers chose the latter

course. Thus, curiously, many one-time isolationist newspapers were among the most positive supporters of the embargo.[28]

    Another frequent objection confronted by the committee
concerned the possibility of inimical repercussions of an
embargo upon American trade. As has been discussed, the
committee replied that the long-term economic gains resulting
from an embargo would far overshadow any losses over the short
run. In any case, it claimed that the two industries most
affected would lose the equivalent of approximately one week's
work during the year through a cessation of the war trade
with Japan. Certainly, it concluded, this was a small price
to pay for justice and America's future security.[29]

    A very prominent public objection to the embargo
concerned the presence of communism in China. Japan was
arguing that by fighting China, she was working to oust
communism from the Far East and thus deserved the support
of the American democracy. On a committee-sponsored motorcade down to Washington in July 1939, the group was frequently "accosted with the proposition that communism was
rampant in China and hence that we should only be grateful
to the Japanese for stamping out this menace." In fact,
this group reported that this "was perhaps the one and only
opposition that we encountered on the road."[30]

    Replies by members of the committee to this sentiment
relied chiefly upon the judgment that the Chinese Communists
were not really Communists. Evans Carlson, in an address
given in Washington, D.C., on February 27, 1940, expressed
this point of view:

        Contrary to popular belief, the group known as
    Chinese Communists are not in fact practicing communism.

> An inspection of the practical application of their
> doctrines convinced the speaker that politically their
> doctrines were representative government, economically
> they could best be described as a glorified cooperative
> society, and socially they could be called communistic
> in the sense that emphasis was placed on the social
> equality of individuals.[31]

Carlson was more sympathetic toward the Chinese Communists
of that period than most committee members, but Price himself
in "Pacific Strategy" casually referred to "the so-called
communist forces (or Eighth Army) in China."[32]

Like members of the committee, many other Americans
of this period, regardless of their political orientations,
considered the Chinese Communists to be austere, dedicated
patriots rather than doctrinaire Communists. This miscon-
ception was widely shared by government leaders; Dorothy Borg
in *The United States and the Far Eastern Crisis of 1933-1938*
concludes, "...American officials as a whole did not achieve
a genuine understanding of the Chinese Communist movement in
the prewar years."[33] In *America's Failure in China, 1941-1950,*
Tang Tsou argues that this inability to comprehend Chinese
communism had its source in the American political tradition
itself, especially in its lack of interest in political
theory.[34]

As the committee's work progressed, the United Front
in China became more a fiction than a reality. As Tang
Tsou reports, "...by the sping of 1940, a pattern of limited
armed conflict and intensive political struggle characterized
the relations between the Kuomintang and the Chinese Communists."
Through 1940 the battles became larger and more frequent,
culminating in the "New Fourth Army Incident" of January 1941.[35]

Although the members of the committee were split in
their support of Chiang Kai-shek vis-à-vis the Communists,
these differences were de-emphasized since they did not
affect the program of the organization. In a letter to
Price on January 16, 1940, Dr. Hume recommended that the
group bring pressure to bear either through the American government or directly upon China to settle the differences between
the Kuomintang and the Communist leaders in China and to maintain unity.[36] But Price, apparently supported by the majority
of the members, felt that it would be preferable for the
committee not to become involved in issues of the civil conflict within China.[37] T.A. Bisson relates how this potentially
disruptive issue was avoided: "I would say that a Judd and
a Communist-inclined member may well have been at odds re
Chiang and the Chinese Communists, but that such differences
were largely plastered over so far as the Committee's activities
were concerned."[38]

Last but not least in the inventory of public objections
to the embargo was the legal objection that though Japan had
broken the Nine-Power Treaty, there was no justification for
the United States, in turn, to break the Treaty of 1911, the
trade agreement with Japan. This problem was automatically
removed, however, on July 26, 1939, when the American government served notice to terminate the Treaty of Commerce and
Navigation between the United States and Japan. After six
months on January 26, 1940, the United States would be legally
free to control or to end its exports or imports with Japan.

In summary, it is remarkable the extent to which the
committee was able to meet all these objections with only
very infrequent recourse to exaggeration or sensationalism.
For all its critics, the committee marshalled political,

economic and legal data to refute their arguments. Emotional-
ism was largely avoided in favor of intellectual proof.

     In government circles the committee met many of the
same objections which it confronted in the nation at large,
as well as several additional doubts of a procedural or
political nature. For example, as it soon discovered, there
was a strong reluctance on the part of Congress to take action
in the field of foreign affairs without a recommendation from
the Department of State.[39] In spite of his strong convictions
on the subject of an embargo, Roger Greene--and, perhaps,
other committee members--felt that such an attitude was
not unreasonable "since the Department is so much better
informed on foreign affairs than the members of Congress can
be."[40] Because of this tendency of Congress to wait for
a lead from the State Department, the committee directed
an increased amount of attention to Secretary Hull and
others in the State Department.
     One of the chief reasons for the government's reluctance to
stop American support to Japan's military effort was the fear of
complications with Japan. Some Congressional and Administration
leaders were afraid that Japan might make war upon the United States
or that the United States might be provoked by a series of
attacks upon Americans to the point at which she would start
a war herself. In answer to a letter from a committee
supporter questioning why, in the face of overwhelming public
demand for a cessation of war shipments to Japan, Congress
still had not acted,[41] Greene replied that, other than a preoccupation with other matters, "fear of unknown complications"
was the primary reason for Congress' failure to pass an embargo.[42]
     In private, however, committee members felt that the

caution of the Administration was due, in part, to a fear
of possible political repercussions from an attempt to secure
an embargo. Certainly, the group had evidence to support this
view. After an interview with Hull in July 1939, Price
reported to Stimson that Hull especially feared that it would
be disastrous both for the Administration and for the country
if an Administration-sponsored embargo bill were to fail to
pass Congress: "If Congress was not really ready to act,
he felt that to stand out alone and be exposed to another
attack and defeat (as in connection with neutrality revision)
might do more harm than good."[43] After an interview with
Hull the following April, Price reported that he still was
reluctant to come out in support of an embargo bill if
there was real danger that it might fail of passage. Before
Hull would lend his public approval to any such legislation,
he wanted to be fairly certain that it had adequate support
in Congress.[44]

Congress, like the Administration, had more than a
healthy respect for the isolationist sentiment of the nation.
Political leaders hesitated to advocate that the United States
take a firmer stand in international affairs for fear of
raising a storm like that stirred up by President Roosevelt
in his famous "Quarantine Speech" of October 1937. Did the
government, however, fail to acknowledge the steady erosion
of isolationism among the American people after that date?
Would the public not have supported more positive efforts
by the United States in international affairs? Obviously,
a definitive answer cannot be given to this question, but
at the time members of the committee certainly believed that
the government was greatly overestimating the rigidity of
isolationist sentiment in America. By the middle of 1939,

public opinion polls indicated that the people had become
less isolationist than their representatives on Capitol Hill,
and during 1940 and 1941 these same polls showed a far
sharper decline of isolationist sentiment among the people
than among their representatives.[45] Slowly, painfully slowly
as far as the committee was concerned, the government awoke
to find itself out of step with the nation and began to take
cautious measures against Japan.

With the aid of historical hindsight, it is possible
to say that the Administration's reluctance to apply more
severe measures to stop American support of Japanese aggression,
though due in part to political considerations, was due more
to a genuine feeling that such measures might lead to war
than the committee believed at the time. Unlike most of the
group's members, Hull seems to have felt that earlier application of compelling economic sanctions, unaccompanied by
American defense commitments in the Far East, would not
deter from her course, but instead would lead her to move
further and faster, especially against the Dutch East Indies,
Indo-China and Singapore. Without the aid of Hull's sources
of intelligence, particularly without Ambassador Grew's
secret messages from Japan, the committee was partially
justified in feeling that the Administration's hesitation
to act was as much due to a recognition of the domestic
political realities as to the exigencies of the international
situation. Nevertheless, Herbert Feis, after a careful
study of the Japanese records, concludes in *The Road to Pearl
Harbor* that an earlier embargo upon the export of American
scrap iron and oil to Japan would have precipitated the
crisis in the Pacific at an earlier date instead of
bringing peace to the area, as members of the committee
continued to believe well into 1940.[46]

Chapter V

SUPPORT

When the campaign began in mid-1938, the American
business community was largely indifferent to America's
role in the Sino-Japanese conflict. Although the group
initially met with very little active opposition to its
efforts from business groups or individuals, only a few
businessmen in mid-1938 were really disturbed over America's
part in Japan's war in China.[1]

In several early National Board meetings, the committee discussed how to enlist the support of American
business in its campaign. Price reflected the sentiment
of the group when he wrote to C.H. French, a prominent
member of the United States Chamber of Commerce: "For a
long time we have felt that we were fighting, in a sense,
a battle for businessmen with inerests in China, as well
as for the broader interests of American security and international confidence and law."[2] The problem for the committee
lay in convincing the business community that it was in its
own best long-range interest for the United States to cease
supporting Japanese aggression in China. To this end it
planned to print and distribute a pamphlet, putting the
issue of non-participation into a realistic perspective
for the business interests concerned.[3] This pamphlet,
however, never materialized; like many other projects it
died for lack of funds. The committee was able to print
a booklet *The Far Eastern Conflict and American Cotton*, which
argued why it was to the advantage of American cotton growers,

shippers, traders and textile manufacturers to stop the flow
of war materials to Japan, but this booklet had little appeal
for non-cotton groups and thus was circulated only among a
limited number of people. To replace the more general pamphlet
for businessmen that was never printed, the organization relied
upon statements from businessmen and interviews and correspondence with the heads of important companies engaged
in trade with Japan.

Within the committee there was a split among the
members with regard to the tenor of its approach toward the
business community. This split was reflected in the members'
reactions to a proposal that the committee print a "black
list" of all American firms continuing to trade with Japan.[4]
Whereas some members ardently supported this suggestion, the
majority objected to the premises on which the idea was based.
This majority preferred to ladle out praise to those firms
which had voluntarily ceased such trade than opprobrium to
those which had not; their counter-proposal was to distribute
a "white list" of firms which had stopped sending war supplies
to Japan. Although this "white list" was never actually printed,
it became a policy of the group to try to enlist the cooperation
of business groups rather than to antagonize them. In its booklet,
America's Share in Japan's War Guilt, one of the recommendations
to organizations wishing to encourage a policy of non-participation
was "to express your moral support to industrialists, merchants,
and other individuals and to labor and other organizations refusing
to cooperate in the manufacture or shipment of supplies for Japan's
war machine."[5]

The committee's approach toward business is indicative
of its entire campaign. With only rare exceptions it sought
to win support for its program through cooperation rather than
vilification. When Price outlined to John D. Rockefeller, Jr.,

his philosophy toward securing business support, he may as
well have been outlining the committee's philosophy toward
its entire campaign:

> There are those who believe that the most effective
> way in which to approach those interests which are doing
> business with Japan in raw materials essential for war
> purposes is to expose and attack them. I like to believe
> that, in the case of enlightened and socially responsible
> leaders like yourself, there is a far better approach
> through frank discussion and thoughtful consideration
> of the tremendously complicated issues involved.[6]

Within the business community the committee found
far more support from individual businessmen than from organized
business groups. It discovered that many important leaders in
such interests as oil and steel were willing to support tacitly,
if not openly, measures to curtail American aid to Japan.[7]
Ernest T. Weir, chairman of National Steel Corporation, cooperated
with the efforts of the committee, but declined an invitation
to become a sponsor;[8] and John D. Rockefeller, Jr., indicated
that he approved of the organization's efforts, but did not
wish to become officially associated with the committee.[9]
Other business figures were willing to participate
openly in the affairs of the committee. The National Board
included three prominent businessmen: E. Snell Hall, vice-
president of Marlin-Rockwell Corporation, manufactures of ball
bearings for automobiles and machines; Frederick C. McKee,
vice-president of West Penn Cement Company and treasurer of
National Casket Company; and A. Merle Hooper, former Standard
Oil representative in China and then president of Papaya
Concentrates Corporation. Hall and Hooper were not active
participants in the committee's work--though both were generous

contributors--but McKee, also chairman of the Committee for
a Boycott Against Aggressor Nations, wrote numerous letters
to various firms, especially oil refineries and airplane manufacturers, asking whether their products were being shipped
to Japan; and he helped in other committee projects directed
toward securing the support of business.

In addition to these National Board members, the group
was able to obtain for one of its honorary vice-chairmen a
former president of the United States Chamber of Commerce--
Henry I. Harriman. Although Harriman was an infrequent parti-
cipant in the committee's affairs, his name lent prestige
to its dealings with the business community. Also on the organization's sponsoring board was the well-known journalist-
turned-businessman Carl Crow, author of *400 Million Customers*.

From organized business groups the committee received
virtually no overt opposition but little public support. The
United States Chamber of Commerce would go no further than
to press the government "to take steps" to remove restrictions
upon American trade in certain regions of China.[10] In May
1939 the Independent Steel and Iron Producers Committee on
Scrap, concerned with shortages of scrap iron and steel in
the United States due to their large export, especially to
Japan, met with Price and agreed to give definite support
to measures for restricting American trade with Japan in
war materials.[11] Such clear backing for the committee's
goals, however, was not common among business groups.

But if these groups rarely supported the committee
openly, they also rarely opposed it openly. When Greene
was asked by a committee supporter whether he thought that
the lobbyists of oil and steel interests were primarily
responsible for the failure of Congress to pass an embargo,[12]

Greene replied that he felt that such forces played only a
very minor role in Washington.[13]   Most of the committee
members agred with Dr. Charles Moser, an economic advisor
in the Department of Commerce, who told Price: "American
businessmen would probably not resent embargo action very
greatly."[14]

The committee found that some of the firms which
were still trading with Japan wished that the government
would stop their trade. Dr. Moser related to Price the
story of one steel manufacturer and exporter who told him:
"I would like to be stopped by the Government."[15] These
manufacturers did not stop exporting voluntarily because
they felt that their unilaterally relinquishing such trade
would only mean that another firm would get the business,
and Japan would be as well supplied as before. As R.E.
McMath, vice-president of the Bethlehem Steel Corporation,
wrote to McKee: "Certainly, if we had not sold them [steel
products] there were plenty of other companies in this
country and elsewhere that would have been glad to do so."[16]
Also, John D. Rockefeller, Jr. pointed out to Greene a
second factor mitigating against a voluntary suspension of
trade by one firm--namely, that it was difficult for a private
corporation to make judgments between two belligerents.[17]

For these reasons the committee found that its efforts
in the business community were again directed to obtaining
an official embargo on exports to Japan. Although a number
of the firms most closely involved in the war trade with Japan
favored restrictions upon such trade, a government embargo--
if only an extension of the "moral embargo"--would be essential
in order to limit decisively this commerce with Japan. This was
the conclusion in *Shall America Stop Arming Japan?*: "For effective

curtailment, government action is necessary."[18]

The committee met with a great deal of emotional
support for the embargo in its relations with organized
labor in the United States; but outside of an enormous number
of resolutions from national and local unions protesting
American aid to Japan, it received little active cooperation
from labor bodies.

Before the committee had been officially organized,
many of the major unions of the country had issued statements
condemning American support of Japan's war on China. The
American Federation of Labor had called for its members and
friends to boycott Japanese goods and services and for "the
democratically governed people [to] stand together refusing
to sell arms and munitions or to make loans to any country
violating international peace and law...."[19] In June 1938
the Industrial Council of the Committee on Industrial Organizations (soon renamed the Congress of Industrial Organizations)
had passed a resolution suporting "an official government
embargo on shipments of war planes, their parts and accessories,
to Japan" and "an immediate embargo on the shipment of oil,
scrap iron and other raw materials of war to Japan."[20] In
the previous October the National Maritime Union of America
had presented to the C.I.O. conference a resolution calling
for an embargo against Japan.[21] Thus, even before the
committee became active, there was strong animus within labor
unions toward America's support of Japan's invasion of China.

But the committee soon discovered that, this animus
nowithstanding, union leaders were reluctant to become
officially connected with the committee. In September 1938
William Green, president of the A.F.L., and John L. Lewis,
president of the C.I.O., both refused invitations to become

sponsors.[22]   At the beginning of the next year, the group
resumed its efforts to enlist labor support, trying to gain the
cooperation of union officials other than Green and Lewis.
Some leaders, like James B. Carey, president of the United
Electrical, Radio and Machine Workers in America and secretary
of the C.I.O., were willing to sign a short statement calling
for America's denial of support to Japan's ruthless government.[23]
But most of the other union officials were hesitant to express
their support for such a statement until the leaders of the two
great union federations had done so.[24]   Acknowledging this
sentiment, the committee in October 1939 once again invited
Green and Lewis to become sponsors, and once again they refused.[25]   The only union figure whom the group ever could
obtain for its sponsoring board was Miss Rose Schneiderman,
president of the National Women's Trade Union League; and both
her participation and usefulness to the committee were negligible.

       In a letter to Roger Greene on October 28, 1939, Price
discussed the committee's efforts with the organized labor movement. He claimed that the "varying response" of labor leaders
was due to at least two factors: "The preoccupation of those
leaders with the internal struggles of labor" and "the fear
of opposition from labor unions in industries which might be
adversely affected by the embargo." Another possible factor
stemmed from the fact that the embargo was being pushed among
the rank and file of labor chiefly by the American League for
Peace and Democracy. Whether the leftist reputation of the
league discouraged many labor leaders from becoming involved
in any group advocating an embargo, Price could not say with
any degree of certainty. He concluded that the chief problem
in the committee's efforts with labor was related to its efforts
on other lines--namely, the lack of time, money and personnel

66

with which to carry on these campaigns.[26] Price's complaint
about lack of funds seems justified in light of the fact
that the often-proposed booklet *The Far Eastern Conflict
and American Labor* was never printed for this reason.

However, the committee's efforts with labor certainly
cannot be dismissed as a failure. In addition to the resolutions of both the A.F.L. and the C.I.O. calling for an
end to American support of Japan's military machine, the
committee in the spring of 1940 printed an eighty-nine page
list of almost two thousand local labor unions protesting aid
to Japan.[27] The fact that many millions of men subject to
military service were willing to advocate that the United
States take measures to stop American economic aid to Japan
indicates that they, like many Americans, did not yet link
the issue of an embargo with the possibility of America becoming involved in war with Japan. These union members reflected a striking and almost universal American naiveté concerning the effect of an embargo upon Japan.

On a personal level the committee was able to maintain
contacts with a number of America's leading newspaper publishers and editors. Among its honorary vice-chairmen were
two of the outstanding men in the field of journalism--William
Allen White, editor of the *Emporia Gazette;* and Jonathan W.
Daniels, editor of the *Raleigh News-Observer*. Serving as a
sponsor was Vincent Sheean, a writer and former newspaperman,
who was highly respected among journalists. With the aid of
these men, the committee was able to broaden its acquaintance-
ships among newspaper editors and to help keep them informed of developments in the Far East, through press releases,
personal letters, interviews and luncheons.

However, the chief influence upon newspaper editorials
remained the news itself rather than interpretations of

it by the committee or any other group. A report of the committee issued on April 7, 1939, assessed candidly the direct
effect of its own publicity upon the newspapers: "The publicity
of the ACNPJA had not had significant effect editorially. Not
more than ten per cent of the papers have responded editorially,
one way or the other."[28] Although its prestige undoubtedly
increased during 1939 and 1940, there is little justification
for claiming that the committee was primarily and directly
responsible for the changes in the attitude of the American
press toward the Far Eastern situation. Whatever the reasons,
though, the group did find that newspaper editorials closely
paralleled the turn in American public opinion; as the American
public came increasingly to support an embargo of war materials
to Japan, newspaper editorials underwent a similar shift toward
advocacy of economic sanctions against her.

In April 1939 the committee conducted its first of two
extensive surveys of American editorial opinion. This report
was based on a study of editorials from 453 daily newspapers
in all 48 states during the period from November 1, 1938, to
April 7, 1939. All editorial opinion had been classified
under one of four headings: those who favored revising the
Neutrality Act for workability, those who favored legislative
action against aggressors, those who favored the Neutrality
Act as it stood then, and those opposed to any discriminatory
action whatever. Those newspapers which fell into either of
the first two groups were classed as internationalist; those
in the last two, as isolationist. This distinction between
internationalist and isolationist, however, is not very useful since, as the committee iself noted, many avowedly
isolationist newspapers specifically supported the embargo.
In any case, the results of the survey showed that 31 per

cent of the newspapers favored Neutrality Law revision and
an additional 46 per cent supported an embargo, while 17
per cent favored the present Neutrality Law and six per
cent opposed any action at all. Thus, as the committee concluded, of the 453 newspapers polled, between 70 and 80 per
cent favored some governmental action to curb American trade
with Japan.[29]

In the fall of 1940, the group conducted its second
survey of American editorial opinion on Far Eastern policy.
This report was based upon 939 editorials dealing with
American policy in the Pacific, taken from 233 newspapers,
published in 105 different cities and towns in 38 states.
The committee found that of the 374 editorials that dealt
with the question of an embargo of exports to Japan, 233
advocated it, only five were opposed, and the remaining
136 mentioned it but were editorially non-committal. (The
report claimed that if deductions were attempted on the basis
of the language used in these "non-committal" editorials,
the proportionate results would not be perceptibly affected.)
Of the 38 editorials that expressed a definite stand upon
an embargo of imports from Japan, 37 favored such action and
only one opposed it. Thus, by December 1940, American newspapers were overwhelmingly in favor of the main objective
of the committeee--to stop American support of Japan's aggressive policy.[30]

Even one of its secondary objectives--American aid
to China--was almost unanimously recommended by American
editors. In a short report based upon the 1940 survey, the
committee analyzed the extent and motivation for this widespread demand for aid to China: "Without exception, American
editors advocate more and immediate aid to China not only
as a matter of moral and treaty obligations, but as sound

strategy because it will probably bring peace to the Pacific without resorting to the use of military force on the part of the U.S."[31]

Interestingly, the possibility of American military force ever being needed in the Pacific was rarely raised by newspaper editors. Some indication of this relative lack of concern for American defense commitments in the Far East can be inferred from the infrequency with which this topic was raised. Although in the 1940 survey 501 editorials dealt with the general question of American moves to resist further Japanese expansion, and 374 specifically discussed the question of embargoing exports to Japan, a scant 48 took up the issue of additional United States bases in the Pacific.[32] As late as December 1940 American newspaper editors, like labor union members and the public in general, did not yet see a vital connection between an American policy of opposing Japanese expansion and the possibility that the United States itself might become involved in war with Japan.

From the beginning of its operations, missionaries and religious leaders played a crucial role in the committee's campaign. Both Harry and Frank Price, as well as several other initial members, had served as missionaries in China. The committee always enjoyed a great deal of support from individual missionary and church leaders, but from the official church organizations and from the mission boards the committee found a more cautious response.

Certainly, among the most enthusiastic supporters of the committee's work were the returned American missionaries who had served in China. Almost to a man, these missionaries ardently advocated an embargo of war supplies to Japan--an embargo that would seriously restrain Japan.[33] After about

1934 the American missionaries in China had become increasingly identified with China and the Chinese people generally and with Chiang Kai-shek and the Nationalist regime specifically,[34] Paul Varg in *Missionaries, Chinese, and Diplomats* writes of this attachment by the missionaries to China: "They had learned to love the people and had come to identify themselves with China. The interests of that nation became their own interests and they were prepared to be their advocates before the world."[35]

When the war broke out again in July 1937 after a four-year interlude of peace, the missionaries took up the cause of China with renewed vigor. Not only did they praise the Chinese people and government, but also they began to demand that the United States extend material assistance to China, particularly by halting the shipment of supplies to Japan. Overcoming the pacifist emotions common among religious leaders of the time, these American missionaries in and from China enthusiastically joined the committee to advocate an American policy of non-participation in Japan's war of aggression in China.[36] Price wrote of these missionaries: "They have played an incalculable part in the work of this Committee."[37]

But, although the missionaries were among the most fervent supporters of the committee's work, the attitude of the mission boards and of the official church organizations was far more equivocal. There were at least two factors operating to prevent these groups from openly encouraging an embargo upon American trade with Japan.

First, there was the problem of American missionaries working in Japan. Many of these missionaries not only staunchly opposed war between the United States and Japan, but also sought to dissuade the United States from taking

economic measures against Japan. The pleas of these missionaries in Japan as well as the concern of the mission boards
for the future of Christianity in Japan served to neutralize
partially the efforts of the missionaries from China.[38] Dr.
Samuel McCrea Cavert, executive secretary of the Federal
Council of Churches, indicated the nature of this problem:
"There were those who, concerned for the Christian movement
in Japan, questioned whether the advantages in China of such
a policy might not be offset by disadvantages in Japan,
including a blame of America and American church people for
the embargo upon war trade."[39]

Second, the isolationist and pacifist inclinations
within the church organizations were another, infinitely
more important, factor in resisting the efforts of the
missionary spokesmen for China. Paul Varg stresses the
strength of this pacifism: "Probably at no time in American
history have so many of the clergy identified war as an
absolute evil to be avoided at all costs, including the cost
of seeing a pagan totalitarianism dominate the world."[40]
Even the Reverend Harry Emerson Fosdick, a sponsor and supporter
of the committee, on May 5, 1940, pledged with a group of
several other illustrious Protestant ministers to take no
part in any way in the Sino-Japanese conflict;[41] and later
the next year Fosdick headed the ministers' No War Committee,
which was financed partly by America First and which sent
noninterventionist literature to 93,000 Protestant ministers.[42]
This craving for peace, so strong among the clergy of this
period, served to nullify the appeal for an embargo against
Japan within the official church bodies.

Although John Masland in "Missionary Influence Upon
American Far Eastern Policy" claims that the missionary movement as a whole advocated a strong policy toward Japan,[43] the

committee's experiences support Varg's contrary contention
that "American missionaries in China were not able to win
over the executives of mission boards to a program of stopping
exports to Japan while continuing to give aid to China."[44]
As Dr. Judd said in the National Board meeting of January 3,
1940, with regard to support for the embargo: "The missionaries see it but the members of the Mission Boards do not."[45]

Indicative of the attitude of these mission boards
was the Foreign Missions Conference of North America with
its large constituency of Protestant missionary organizations.
Throughout the period encompassed by the work of the committee,
the conference vacillated over its policy with regard to the
Sino-Japanese conflict. As Varg notes, the very real sympathy
for China had to be reconciled with the powerful conviction
that the United States should not become involved. As a result,
the conference condemned Japan's barbarism in China and called
for a voluntary embargo of American war supplies to Japan,
but it refused to advocate an official government embargo.[46]
In a letter to Price in May 1939, A.L. Warnshuis, an executive
of the conference, indicated that he felt that an embargo unaccompanied by a willingness to intervene militarily would
be ineffective as a check against Japan and would only antagonize
her.[47] To the sorrow of the committee, the Foreign Missions
Conference never came to support its program.

The committee was similarly disappointed in its relations with the Federal Council of Churches of Christ in
America, which served as an interorganizational council for
twenty-six Protestant denominations with a total membership
of more than twenty-two million. On June 3, 1938, the Executive
Committee passed a resolution condemning the bombing of civilian
populations in China and Spain and recommending that the churches

urge their members to "yield the profits derived from the sale
of munitions to all nations and especially to those who in-
vade the homelands of other peoples with armed force...."
Secretary Hull, the resolution concluded, should "use his
influence to persuade those concerned who are now selling
war supplies to discontinue voluntarily such practice."[48]
Yet, the Federal Council never officially supported a government embargo against Japan, even though it recommended a
similar embargo against Russia a few days after Finland had
been invaded.[49] The fear of war with Japan continued to
overshadow the Federal Council's sympathy for the Chinese
people.

Many of the committee members would have agreed with
Dr. Judd in speaking of the caution and fear of the Protestant Church as "the greatest tragedy"[50] or with Price
in raising the question of a "lack of moral courage" within
the church in America.[51] The dearth of support for the
embargo from within the Protestant Church upholds Varg's
conclusion that "American Protestantism as a whole backed
away from assuming any responsibility to help halt totalitarianism...."[52]

Although the committee failed to win the approval
of many of the important national church organizations, it
did have the cooperation of others. The World Alliance
for International Friendship Through the Churches, a group
of clergymen of the Protestant, Catholic and Jewish faiths,
passed a resolution explicitly advocating passage of an
embargo against Japan. Other such groups supporting an
embargo included the General Conference of the Methodist
Episcopal Church, South, the National Convention of the
Young Women's Christian Association and, after June 1939,

the General Assembly of the Presbyterian Church in the
United States.[53]

The committee found its greatest support within the
American religious community, however, not from any national
organizations but from individuals and local groups.[54] Dr.
Robert E. Speer, former president of the Federal Council
of Churches, was one of the original honorary vice-chairmen.
The National Board included such religious leaders as Dr.
Judd, Professor Reinhold Niebuhr and Dr. Henry Pitt Van Dusen,
president of the Union Theological Seminary. Among the
committee's sponsors were over twenty important figures
in American religion, such as Dr. Fosdick, Dr. E. Stanley
Jones, the well-known missionary to India, Dr. Henry Smith
Leiper, foreign secretary of the Federal Council of Churches,
Dr. William Pierson Merrill, president of the Church Peace
Union, the Right Reverend G. Ashton Oldham, Bishop of Albany
and president of the World Alliance for International Friendship, and Dr. Stephen S. Wise, Rabbi of the Free Synagogue.
These and other leaders in American religion helped to balance,
at least in part, the disappointing failure of most of the
official religious organizations to oppose actively America's
role in Japan's military aggression in China.

Chapter VI

TERMINATION

The passage of the National Defense Act on July 2,
1940, marked the beginning of the end of the committee's
campaign. Public opinion was almost unanimously in favor
of an embargo upon exports of war materials to Japan, and the
legislative authority had been secured for the President to
act to withhold this trade. In a series of proclamations beginning on July 2, President Roosevelt placed an increasing
number of commodities, including munitions, machinery and
oil, under severe export restrictions. Many leaders of the
committee felt that the Administration and the committee
were in very close agreement as to goals with their differences
involving only such aspects as timing and tempo. Having
helped to gain the support of both the general public and the
government for its program of non-participation in Japanese
aggression, the organization felt that it was time to consider
terminating its efforts.

In the National Board meeting of June 3, 1940, the
question of the future course of the committee was raised.
During the ensuing discussion, several members--notably, Dr.
B.A. Garside, Dr. Edward Hume and Edgar Rue--felt that the
committee should direct its efforts increasingly toward helping
in Chinese reconstruction. A smaller group of individuals
led by Philip Jaffe instead advocated that it reorient itself
into a foreign policy action organization concentrating upon the
Far Eastern situation. A third group felt that it should simply
close down once it was apparent that its original goals had
been substantially met. As the discusson ended, Price recommended

that the members, while following through on the present program until it had been carried as far toward realization as
possible, consider the alternatives already mentioned, chiefly:
"(1) Reorganizing as an American committee for cooperating
with China or as an American committee on Pacific Reconstruction;
(2) Reorganizing in combination with other organizations for
the establishment of a strong national foreign policy action
organization."[1]

In the weeks that followed this meeting, Price weighed
alternative courses for the future of the committee. On June 8
in a letter to Henry Luce, Price wrote that several members,
especially Garside and himself, as well as some unofficial
advisors like Edward C. Carter and Dr. Edward C. Lobenstine,
"have come to the view that, if and as the 'non-participation'
effort is less needed, there should be a reorientation toward
positive aid for fundamental reconstruction in China." Price
hoped that the committee could study the channels through
which this aid could be directed and could help to coordinate
and mobilize these efforts in America, so that long-term
assistance to China could be realized.[2]

A week later, however, in a letter to Greene, Price
described a recent conversation with Henry Stimson in which
he had proposed to Stimson the formation of a "general organization working for public support of a sound and constructive
foreign policy." Price admitted to Greene that he himself
was coming to favor such a reorientation: "I confess that
this and other recent conversations have led me to swing more
in the direction of our putting our full energy into such
a general organization."[3]

But Price still felt that the problems involved in
such a reorganization of the group's efforts were serious

and must not be minimized.[4] In fact, the gravity of
these problems was to increase in Price's mind over the next
few weeks until he came to believe that it would be preferable
to terminate the committee rather than to try to reorient it.

At the next meeting of the National Board on October 21,
1940, the question of the future of the committee was once
again discussed. In the preceding months the majority of the
members, including Price and Greene, had come to the view that
rather than try to redirect its efforts toward fresh goals,
the committee should simply cease its campaign in the near
future. A termination, it was felt, would leave the way open
for: "(1) Possible formation of a strong national committee
concerned primarily with greatly increased aid to China.
(2) Other organizations like the Committee to Defend America
to increase their emphasis upon the Far Eastern situation."[5]

As the members all knew, both of these programs were
well under way by that time. First, beginning in September,
Dr. Garside had been communicating with Price, Luce and
others interested in the future of China over the possibility
of consolidating the various China agencies into a single
organization devoted to China relief; these efforts were to
culminate in the formation of United China Relief at the beginning of 1941. Second, the Committee to Defend America
by Aiding the Allies, formed back in May, had begun to spend
more time on the Far Eastern question, having adopted the
embargo against Japan as one of its objectives.

The activity of these other groups was only one of
several factors behind the decision of the majority of the
members to recommend closing down the operation of the
committee. These members also felt that any reorientation
would require a massive new effort, new organization, new

backing, and possibly a new executive secretary since Price
indicated that he might not be available.[6] More fundamentally,
several members feared that to direct the committee's efforts
toward a new goal would constitute manipulation of the present
supporters, many of whom had affiliated with the committee
solely in order to realize its "single and central aim...'non-
participation in Japanese aggression.'"[7] The majority of
the group, thus, believed that a reorientation would be un-
necessary, impractical and perhaps even unethical.

A minority of the members, an influential and
vociferous though not numerous minority, passionately resisted
the proposal to terminate the activities of the committee.
Where the minutes of the October 21 meeting record "some
differences of opinion" over the issue,[8] Harry Price recalls
that this disagreement over the question of closing the
committee was heated and serious--the nearest the organization
ever came to a substantive argument. The minority, as Price
relates, pressed for a "reorientation and perpetuation of our
Committee as a central organization working to mobilize
American public opinion in support of 'enlightened' policies
vis-à-vis China and other parts of Asia."[9]

For these people the Committee to Defend America
was anything but an advocate of such a policy. Frederick V.
Field, an unofficial advisor to the committee, who was
chairman of *Amerasia*--on which Jaffe was managing editor and
Bisson, a member of the Editorial Board--wrote Price criticizing the doctrine "of the William Allen White Committee to the
effect that Great Britain, as well as China, is fighting
democracy's battles. This I thoroughly disagree with...."[10]
Rather than ally with Great Britain, an aging imperialist
power, the United States should seek closer cooperation with

the Soviet Union. Although Field was more open in his pro-
Soviet and anti-British inclinations than any of his associates
on the committee, there was a strong minority who were anxious
to convert the organizaton into a foreign policy action group
far different from the White Committee to Defend America.

The very fact that there was serious disagreement
within the National Board over new alternative policies
served to convince many members that the time had come for
the committee to terminate the organization. Until that
time it had enjoyed the full cooperation of its members so
long as it had concentrated upon its original function--to
stop American participation in Japanese aggression. Now,
as the Board debated perpetuating the organization for a broader
campaign, the extent of the differences among members became
increasingly evident and crucially important. How the committee should act in relation to China's tenuous United Front
had been largely ignored in the past since this matter was
not central to the group's efforts; but, if the committee
were to advocate an extensive American policy toward the Far
East, the issue of Chiang Kai-shek vis-à-vis the Communists
would come to be of great significance. On this one issue
there was such dissent among various members that an agreement on policy probably would never have been reached, at
least without alienating a large number of supporters. Rather
than attempt to decide upon a new direction for the committee,
the majority concluded that it would be better to terminate
its efforts once its original purpose had been largely achieved.
And, by the fall of 1940, most members felt that while the
embargoes were still far from complete, the principles on
which they were based had been well recognized, and further
progress would come without the necessity for large public
agitation.[11]

During the meeting of October 21, 1940, the decision
was reached to wait until after the November elections had
passed before setting a fixed time for closing.[12] For the
next three months the committee continued its efforts, sending
out press releases and analyses dealing with extensions of
the embargo and corresponding with its members and friends.
However, this campaign was carried on at a much diminished
pace; as early as July 4, 1940, the full-time staff had been
reduced from its peak of nineteen to a mere three.[13] Through
December several members, particularly Greene and Schain,
pressed for a liquidation of the committee in the very near
future. At the beginning of January, Price proposed a con-
cluding drive by the committee during that month: "...there
should be one final, vigorous effort to secure further extensions in the embargo upon war supplies to Japan, as well
as to give the strongest possible support to developments
now under consideration on behalf of further aid to China."[14]
This last effort never materialized, however, and on February
1, 1941, the committee ended its active campaign--"in the
black," as Harry Price proudly recalls.[15]

At the final National Board meeting, it had been
decided to maintain a small committee, consisting of Price,
Greene, Garside and Hume, as an Ad Interim Policy and Action
Committee to continue to carry on after February 1 in line
with the stated policy of the committee.[16] In John Masland's
"Missionary Influence Upon American Far Eastern Policy,"
printed in September 1941, he noted that this small action
committee was still operating: "...they continue to maintain
a skeleton organization which could be called upon once again
were conditions to warrant."[17] In fact, this skeleton organization did not actually function as any sort of official

group; to all intents and purposes the campaign of the
American Committee for **Non-Participation** in Japanese Aggression
ceased on February 1, 1941.

In the final National Board meeting the committee
also had decided to divide its papers into three groups.
The accumulated papers, correspondence and literature, as
well as the resource file, were turned over to the Littauer
Center of Public Administration at Harvard University; the
card file of 30,000 active supporters went to United China
Relief, Inc.; and the Congressional file containing correspondence with members of Congress, records of positions
taken by individual Congressmen with reference to **America's**
Far Eastern policy, **and copies of pertinent bills** was trans-
ferred to Roger Greene, who had become active in the Committee
to Defend America.[18]

When the committee disbanded, most if its members
returned to their respective careers. Since work with the
organization had not been a full-time job for most of them,
since the committee had been but one of their many affiliations
and interests, its closing hardly signified a turning-point
in any of their lives.

After sifting **through a vari**ety of offers, Harry
Price chose to become active **in the Council for** Democracy,
a group of scholars studying the basic **features** of American
democracy. Soon after the passage of the Lend-Lease Bill
in March 1941, Price left the council to become treasurer
and a **director of China Defense Supplies, Inc.,** which assisted
the Chinese Nationalist **Government** in its Lend-Lease negotia-
tions. From 1944 to 1947 he served as assistant director
in the China Mission of the United Nations Relief and Re-
habilitation Administration and wrote the Far Eastern part

of its three-volume official history in 1948. After the
Communist take-over of mainland China in 1949, Price worked
in the European Division of the Economic Cooperation Administration and its successor, the Mutual Security Agency, in
charge of programming Marshall Plan aid to the dependent overseas territories of Western European nations. In 1955 after
three years of research, he completed *The Marshall Plan and
Its Meaning*, a definitive study of the Marshall Plan, written
at the behest of the government. Since that time he has served
as economic advisor to the **government** of Nepal, as executive
director of the International Mass Education Movement, and
as director of Technical Cooperation and Publications of
the International Institute of Rural Reconstruction in the
Philippines. At the beginning of 1967, Price resigned from
the institute in order to devote his time to further writing.[19]

After the committee's termination Roger Greene
became increasingly active in the Committee to Defend America.
As early as July 2, 1940, he had written to a friend, "At
present I am fully occupied with work for the Committee to
Defend America by Aiding the Allies...."[20] With the liquida-
tion of the American Committee, Greene simply continued with
the White Committee, as associate director. During most of
World War II he served as an economic consultant in the
Division of Cultural Relations of the Department of State.
He died at his home in Worcester, Massachusetts, in 1947.

Dr. B.A. Garside went on to become executive director
and then vice-president and secretary of United China Relief,
Inc., the organization which he had helped to create in the
fall of 1940. By the end of 1941, most of the China relief
groups had pooled their efforts into United China Relief,
which undertook a systematic, nationwide campaign on behalf

of aid to China that continued through World War II.[21]
In the years that have followed the war, Dr. Garside has
continued to be active in a variety of philanthropic organizations dealing with the Far East and especially Nationalist
China. Currently, he is executive director of the American
Bureau for Medical Aid to China, executive vice-chairman of
the American Emergency Committee for Tibetan Refugees, and
executive director of Aid to Refugee Chinese Intellectuals.[22]

Like Dr. Garside, other members of the committee
returned to their previous careers and affiliations after
the committee terminated its campaign. Josephine Schain
maintained her activities in various national and international women's organizations such as the Pan-Pacific
Women's Association; she is now retired in New York City.
Dr. Edward H. Hume continued to work with overseas medical
missions until his death in 1957. Maxwell Stewart remained
as associate editor of *The Nation* until 1947, and he con-
tinues to serve as secretary of the Public Affairs Committee
and as editor of *Public Affairs Pamphlets*.

Major Evans Carlson published his well-known study,
The Chinese Army: Its Organization and Military Efficiency,
in 1941. With the beginning of the war, he reenlisted in
the Marines, founding and leading the famed Marine unit
later known as Carlson's Raiders. Wounded in action,
Carlson suffered from progressively poorer health until his
death in 1947.

Late in 1940 Dr. Walter Judd moved to Minneapolis
to return to the practice of medicine; but at the
behest of friends, he ran for a seat in the United States
Congress in 1942. Easily defeating his opponent, Judd
remained in the House for ten terms, becoming a leader in
the Republican party and a prominent figure in the "China

bloc," a group of pro-Chiang critics of the Administration's foreign policy after World War II.[23] More than any other man, Judd helped to build up a tremendous following for Chiang in the United States.[24] Since retiring from Congress in 1963, Dr. Judd has maintained a full lecture schedule both in this country and abroad, speaking primarily on the Far East.[25]

Several other ex-members of the committee joined Dr. Judd in attacking America's postwar policy in China and especially in advocating greatly increased aid to the Chinese Nationalist Government. The American China Policy Association, the most active of the organizations which were established for the specific task of promoting aid to Chiang, had among its active members Mrs. George Fitch and Freda Utley, in addition to Dr. Judd.[26] Two other oganizations, founded for the express purpose of exerting pressure for greater American aid to China, operated between 1949 and 1952; in both the China Emergency Committee and the Committee to Defend America by Aiding Anti-Communist China, Frederick C. McKee played an instrumental role, serving as chairman of the two groups.[27]

Meanwhile, other leaders in the American Committee for Non-Participation in Japanese Aggression assumed quite different roles in the postwar political debate on China. Philip Jaffe continued to work as managing editor of *Amerasia* until the magazine's demise in July 1947. In 1945 Jaffe was convicted and fined for accepting several hundred classified documents from government officials such as John S. Service, a career Foreign Service officer in the Department of State, for use in *Amerasia*. In the course of the inquiry, Jaffe's extensive dealings with the Communist party headquarters in

New York and its leaders as well as with the Soviet Embassy were revealed. In 1952 Senator Joseph R. McCarthy used this episode in highly publicized investigations of alleged Communist infiltration into the government.[28]

T.A. Bisson, as an associate of Jaffe, also was involved in the McCarthy investigations as well as in the hearings of Senator Pat McCarran's Senate Subcommittee on Internal Security. Bisson came under sharp criticism for the highly complimentary picture which he had painted of Chinese Communism in an article in 1943 in *Far Eastern Survey*.[29] Like Philip Jaffe and Maxwell Stewart, Bisson was included in a list in the report of the McCarran Subcommittee as among those "identified as members of the Communist Party."[30] From 1948 to 1953 he was a special lecturer on the Far East at the University of California, and since 1956 he has been chairman of Intercultural Studies at the Western College for Women in Oxford, Ohio.[31]

As the committee's members moved into ever-widening circles after 1941, it became increasingly apparent that the organization had contained an extraordinarily diverse group of people. While some of its leaders such as Judd, McKee, Mrs. Fitch and Miss Utley were considered part of the so-called "China lobby," others like Jaffe, Bisson and Stewart assumed very different roles. The same people who in the late 1930's and 1940 had been able to cooperate closely on the issue of non-participation in Japanese aggression came to occupy widely spaced positions on the postwar political spectrum. Harry Price's view, as early as June 1938, that the organization should direct its efforts solely toward its initial, precisely defined goal in order to retain the support of its members was vindicated by the political fragmentation of the membership of the committee following its termination.

Chapter VII

EVALUATION

Certainly, the efforts of the committee had a significant effect both upon American public opinion and upon
American policy toward the Far Eastern crisis. In both areas
important changes occurred during its two-and-a-half-year
campaign. But how many of these developments can be traced
to the work of the committee? To what extent was the committee itself, rather than other groups and other factors,
responsible for the shift in the American public's attitude
toward the proper role of the United States in Far Eastern
affairs, and to what extent was the committee responsible
for the incorporation of this shift in public attitude into
American policy?

No satisfactory answers can be obtained to these
questions. To attempt to define the roots of public opinion
on any issue as complex as American attitudes toward the
Far East is an overwhelming task that can yield only specu-
lative and debatable results. That the committee played
some role in the evolution of American opinion on the subject
is indisputable, but how large a role it played is unanswer-
able. In this period, as in other periods, the most decisive
influence upon American public opinion was that of the events
themselves as they unfolded in Asia and Europe. As Harry
Price willingly states, the mere course of events in Asia
was probably a greater factor in warning the American people
of the threat of Japan than anything that the committee did.[1]
The greatly improved newspaper, newsreel, and radio reporting,
aided by developments in technology, served to bring the news

of the world directly and literally into the living rooms
of America.

But, important as these events in themselves might
be, there had to be individuals and organizations to inter-
pret them, to analyze the trends beneath them, and to relate
them meaningfully to the concerns of the nation. For the
first year of the Sino-Japanese conflict, there existed no
such organization, and, partially as a result, American public
opinion remained uninformed and confused on the issue.[2] Of
course, most Americans deplored Japan's brutal invasion of
China; but how was this conflict related to America, and, in
any case, what could America do?

The committee took this substantial public sympathy
for China--as early as October 1937 polls indicated that
59 per cent of the American people were "pro-China" as against
only one per cent that were "pro-Japan"[3]--and focused it upon
the danger that Japanese expansion presented not only to China,
but to the United States as well. It helped to mold this relatively detached compassion for China into active support of
a government policy of resisting Japan through nonmilitary
measures. By June 1939 the percentage of Americans sympathetic
to China had risen to 74 per cent,[4] but more significantly
72 per cent were in favor of an embargo upon the export of
war materials to Japan, and within two months this second
figure was to rise to 82 per cent.[5] From polls such as these,
as well as from the flood of resolutions, letters, and tele-
grams directed to Washington, it is apparent that the overwhelming majority of Americans came to support legislative
or executive action to stop the sale of war supplies to Japan.

Evaluating the influence of the work of the committee
upon government policy is no easier than evaluating its effect

upon public opinion. Administration leaders, then or later, were not anxious to explain precisely what factors motivated them to advocate specific policies. Nevertheless, the committee felt, with some justification, that its efforts had contributed toward a series of steps taken by the government against Japan, indirectly by creating a mood of popular acceptance of sterner government action and directly through personal interviews and correspondence with leaders of the government.[6]

The committee could point to a variety of measures that were attributable in some degree to its efforts: the adoption and extension of the moral embargo, beginning in June 1938 with its appeal to the makers and exporters of aircraft, aircraft parts, engines, armaments, aerial bombs and torpedoes, the denunciation of the 1911 commercial treaty with Japan on July 26, 1939, Ambassador Grew's warning to the Japanese people on October 19, 1939, that the Japanese army must abandon its aggressive policies if Japan was to avoid trouble with the United States, the granting of additional loans and credits to China, the passage of the National Defense Act on July 2, 1940, and its implementation in a series of Presidential proclamations.[7] In addition to these successes, the committee could point to its support of the Pittman and Schwellenbach embargo bills in Congress, which, though never passed, helped to keep the issue squarely before the American government. In the case of all these measures, the committee played some role, large or small, direct or indirect. Although the Administration would never, of course, tell the committee to what extent American policy was a response to its demands, Secretary Hull's repeated encouragement to Price and Greene indicates that he believed the group to be serving an essential role in preparing the American people to accept a more positive policy in the Far East.

As difficult as it is to assess precisely the
influence of the committee, "there is sufficient evidence
to believe that it has been considerable," as an historian
writing shortly after its termination concluded.[8] Its work
was a significant factor in overcoming the indifference and
isolationism across the country and in Congress with regard
specifically to the Sino-Japanese conflict and generally to
the role of the United States in world affairs.

Although the committee initially avoided linking
its efforts to the European situation, it found that
America's Far Eastern policy could not be treated independent-
ly of its policy in Europe and that, accordingly, the non-
participation program could not be divorced from the European
conflict. In its contact with the question of the proper role
of the United States in world affairs, as against purely
Asian ones, the committee discovered a curious tendency on
the part of the American people, a tendency also observed
by historians: Americans were willing to accept greater
responsibilities earlier in the Far East than in Europe.[9]
In the report of its motorcade to Washington in July 1939,
this greater readiness to act in Asia was noted: "While
it was all too evident to all concerned that American public
opinion was definitely divided on the subject of European
policy, it seemed fairly evident...that American public
opinion was extraordinarily united on the subject of American
participation in Japanese aggression."[10]

Why was this so? First, the chain of aggression had
begun earlier in Asia than in Europe; the Manchurian crisis
of 1931 preceded any similar European conflict by several
years. The American public, then, was given a longer period
of time in which to focus its attention on the threat of
Japanese expansion. Second, there was a century-old tradition

of American friendship for China, unparalleled by any such
sentiment for a European nation. Third, Japan, unlike any
European power, did not have a large number of emigrants in
the United States.[11] As a result, practically the only group
defending the Japanese point of view in America was the
missionaries who had returned from Japan, and their influence
was very limited. Fourth, the ideological issues were not
as complex in Asia as in Europe; virtually no Americans
harbored either affection or respect for the government of
Japan, whereas more than a few felt this way toward Hitler
or Mussolini. Fifth, Americans were so preoccupied with
President Roosevelt's anti-German moves that they were much
more willing to give him a free hand in Asia than in Europe.
Organizations such as America First paid so little attention
to the Far Eastern situation that they voiced relatively
slight opposition to the steps that were taken that led to
the impasse preceding Pearl Harbor.[12] Sixth, a strong policy
in the Far East did not involve the cooperation with England
that many Americans feared in the case of European intervention.[13] Seventh, Japan was never considered as formidable
an opponent as Germany. Within this last attitude was a strong
element of racial superiority; Americans could not bring themselves to believe that a non-Caucasian race could ever be a
real threat to a major power.[14]

This greater willingness of Americans to take a strong
stand against Japan as against Germany enabled the American
government to establish precedents for such a policy that soon
could be applied to the European crisis. As Price recalled
in September 1942 of the committee's campaign, it "did succeed
in helping to crack the isolationist front on one clear-cut
issue...."[15] When to this first crack was added the rents

created by America's European policy, America's monolithic isolationism began to crumble.

Although directed almost exclusively to the Asian conflict, then, the work of the committee yielded results that were relevant to the European situation. America's involvement in Asia preceded and to some extent facilitated her involvement in Europe and the world at large.

In the period that began with the initiation of the committee's campaign and ended with the termination of the Second World War, American thinking about foreign policy, military strategy and world organization underwent significant and lasting changes. Harry Price recalls those years during which the committee operated: "It was a period of transition in the thinking of many Americans about the interdependence of nations and the role of the United States in international affairs, and that is a characteristic of the history of those years that was of particular interest to members of the Committee."[16] The committee occupies a crucial position in the historic evolution of American attitudes toward inter-national affairs. It represents a transitional stage between isolationism and internationalism; it served as a bridge between two polar conceptions of America's role in the com-munity of nations.

By focusing on one vivid, inescapable issue--American support to Japan's military machine--by leading the American people to think specifically about this one issue, the com-mittee encouraged Americans to examine and define the interests of the United States, both material and moral, in the Far East. Since Americans have never been emotional isolationists, never able to purge themselves of curiosity and compassion for people in distant lands, the committee had relatively little difficulty in convincing the American people that they did have important reasons for wanting to see an end to Japan's expansion at the expense of China.

To this argument that America did have significant interests in the Far East was added the fact that the United States, whether it wanted to or not, would play a crucial role in the Sino-Japanese conflict: If it continued to trade with Japan, it would be aiding her; if it stopped, it would be aiding China. As Americans defined the issue in these terms, they began to seek an affirmative and intelligent policy with which to handle the problem in a manner consistent with both self-interest and justice. The shibboleths of isolationism were tacitly laid aside as numerous isolationists conceded that America simply had to construct some consistent policy in the Far East. The committee was extremely fortunate to have at hand a program that could appeal to these quasi-isolationists as well as to the internationalists.

To understand the remarkably widespread popularity of the committee's policy, one must recognize that there have been two contradictory heritages in America's attitude toward the world. On the one hand, there is the tradition of isolationism, the avoidance of participation in alliances, engagements or conflicts with other nations. On the other hand, there is the tradition of American concern for a free and democratic world.[17] As strong as isolationism ever became in the 1930's, it never completely overshadowed the conviction that, as Ralph Waldo Emerson wrote, "the office of America is to liberate."[18] America's diplomatic history can be extensively interpreted in terms of the shifting resolution between these two conflicting heritages.

While isolationism was so pervasive during the

1930's, Americans could satisfy the imperatives of their second
tradition by claiming that **America could serve as an example**
to the rest of the world, that the American democracy could
set a standard for people of other lands. To some extent,
this method was buttressed by occasional moral and legal
pronouncements which sought to bring the weight of public
opinion down upon transgressing nations. However, as the
interest of Americans in maintaining a world of peace and
freedom rather than one of war and totalitarianism grew,
merely setting a passive example for the rest of the world
or voicing disregarded platitudes no longer seemed sufficient.
Americans unconsciously sought some means of taking a larger,
more active role in **international** affairs, but always in the
context that America must remain at peace. **Involvement in**
world affairs but never at the expense of war--this was the
silent striving of many Americans as the committee was organized
in mid-1938.

        Its **members,** reflecting the same **inner tension that**
marked the general public, discovered an American policy that
satisfied almost perfectly the goal of limited involvement
for which many Americans yearned. **Non-participation in Japanese**
aggression--here at last was a **decisive,** intelligent policy
for America that would not entail military intervention.
Stop sending American war supplies to Japan, said the committee: "We would be doing our part now in a more courageous
and realistic way toward laying new foundations for world
peace."[19] Here, **paradoxically,** the United States could make
a definite **contribution toward** the maintenance of international
law and order by isolating itself, by ceasing to **trade in**
war supplies with Japan.

        The strong isolationist current of the country was

mirrored in the committee's first booklet *America's Share in Japan's War Guilt*. The cry of the isolationists to "get the profits out of war," that had resulted in the Neutrality Act of 1937, was paraphrased on the booklet's cover: "Take American war profits out of Japan's aggression in China."[20] Not surprisingly, in one of its earliest meetings, the committee had discussed possible cooperation with other groups on the basis of such objectives as "U.S. avoidance of entangling alliances likely to lead to war."[21] Although the vast majority of the group's members were not themselves isolationists, they were aware that the program that they were advocating would have strong appeal to such people.

Rather than doctrinaire isolationists, the mass of Americans were noninterventionists; they hoped for the defeat of totalitarianism, but not at the expense of American military involvement.[22] For such people the policy of the committee was ideal. The United States could make its weight felt in the Sino-Japanese conflict by foregoing certain advantages-- particularly the profits from her war-time trade with Japan-- yet without assuming the risk of going to war.

The policy of non-participation was especially popular among Americans because it was moral, it was just. Continuing to export supplies that would be used to further military aggressions was wrong; it meant that the United States itself was taking a side in the war. From the beginning of its campaign, the committee struck this chord of American guilt for her role in Japan's war. The very title of its booklet, *America's Share in Japan's War Guilt* assigned a portion of Japan's culpability to America. Within the pamphlet was the implication that enacting an embargo against Japan would absolve America: "Whatever other nations may do, our consciences then will be

clear."[23] In December 1939, the group again hinted that a
non-participation program would eliminate America's role in
the war: "We have laid out a program which, if it can be
put through, will probably take America out of this war...."[24]
Actually, most of its members did not want, in any complete
sense, "to take America out of this war"; many would have
welcomed a placing of America's economy, though never its
military, on the side of China. But the thought of taking
America out of a war, any war, had tremendous psychological
appeal at a time in which pacifism was such a powerful force;
and the committee, preoccupied with the terminating of aid
to Japanese militarism, sometimes argued in such terms.

But if the committee was to continue to occupy its
narrow position between isolationism and internationalism,
it would have to emphasize that its program would be unlikely
to bring America into a war and that it was not advocating
military intervention. These very arguments, in fact, were
repeated time and time again, especially in 1939 and the early
months of 1940. These assurances, reflecting generally the
views of the committee's members, were apparently considered
essential; for most Americans of this period had to be con-
vinced, before they would support any kind of American involvement in world affairs, that such involvement would not
lead to war.

Some members of the committee did a superb job of
minimizing the danger of war--so superb, in fact, that they
succeeded in convincing themselves. President Roosevelt employed a strategy similar to that of the committee when he
continually played down the risks inherent in a policy of
all-out aid for the Allies against the Axis in order to keep
the isolationists at bay while he put the material resources
of the country at the disposal of Germany's opponents.[25]

But, where documents prove that Roosevelt was aware that he
was deceiving the public, albeit for a worthy goal, the records
that survive do not indicate a similar benevolent duplicity
on the part of the committee. In neither its literature nor
its correspondence is there any inkling that it was artfully
de-emphasizing the danger of war in order to win the support
of Americans for its program. Until mid-1940 there is no data
to support any other conclusion than that the vast majority of
its members honestly believed there was no substantial danger
of war with Japan as a consequence of the imposition of an
embargo on war supplies from the United States.

The risk of war seemed so slight that the committee
almost never spoke of what the United States should do if
an embargo did not stop Japanese expansion, if instead it
incited the Japanese to move further and faster. In a session
of the Senate Committee on Foreign Relations in April 1939,
Senator Vandenberg asked Dr. Judd precisely this question:
What ought the United States to do if an embargo only made
Japan more offensive to America? Judd replied: "I just
won't go to war under any circumstances, because going to
war would not make it any better, it would make it worse."
Earlier, he had indicated to the Senate Committee to just
what extent he objected to any kind of American military
involvement in Asia: "We ought to decide and declare flatly
to the world that we will defend our soil and possessions
and the Western Hemisphere from European or Asiatic encroach-
ments, but that we will not send our armies or navies to
Europe or Asia to defend a foot of anyone else's territory
or any status quo there; that we will not allow our goods to
be transported into any war zone while still our goods are
in our ships...."[26] In retrospect, it seems certain that such

a flat assurance to the Japanese would largely vitiate any
inhibitory effect of an embargo upon Japanese expansion.
In fact, about the only real benefit of an embargo combined
with a declaration like that of Judd would be to salve the
conscience of America by removing her responsibility for
supporting economically Japan's aggression.

This type of approach would not have been inconsistent
with America's traditional policy toward China--a split between
humanitarianism and strategic realism. In *American Diplomacy*
George F. Kennan emphasizes America's general inadvertence
toward power politics in its Far Eastern policy:

> We see a distinct difference between our policy
> toward this area and our policy toward Europe....We find
> ourselves more willing to accept involvement in oriental
> affairs, less inclined to dismiss them as of no moment
> to us. On the other hand, we find no greater readiness,
> so far, to admit the validity and legitimacy of power
> realities and aspirations....[27]

In mid-1939 few people saw any logical inconsistency
between a policy of resisting Japanese expansion economically
and one of refusing to oppose it militarily. A.L. Warnshuis
of the Foreign Missions Conference, however, pointed to this
contradiction in one of the committee's statements, Dr. Speer's
circular letter to ministers: "In the first paragraph you
ask us to appeal to our Government to protest the sale of
materials for military use by Japan, but in the second paragraph you, in effect, protest against any military intervention."
After conceding that a discriminatory embargo may not lead to
war, he argued that the committee must be prepared to face this
consequence. Warnshuis cautioned: "To say in advance that

you do not want any military interference is to stultify
yourself and to nullify the request you are making."[28]
In the same vein, Senator Robert A. Taft, in response to
Roosevelt's Lend-Lease proposal, concluded that if one granted
the President's premise that American security warranted
the spending of large sums of money to defend Britain, then
logically the United States was obliged to enter the war
herself.[29]

To Warnshuis, Price replied that the danger of an
embargo leading to war was so slight that the committee
did not consider it necessary to advocate military measures.[30]
What Price did not say was that to suggest or even discuss
American military involvement in the Far East, under any
circumstances, would be to take an enormous step away from
isolationism, a step that would split the committee and
alienate many of its supporters. Most Americans of this
period wanted to believe that totalitarianism could be
stopped without American military intervention, and they
supported the committee partly because it did not undercut
this illusion. If the group were to raise the possibility
of America having to go to war, many of these people would
cease their participation in the committee rather than
repudiate their illusion.

Through 1939 the committee continued to speak of its
non-participation program as a "middle course" between the
two extremes of drift and active military intervention.[31]
Never did it suggest that there was any likelihood of
military involvement in the Far East, regardless of what
Japan might do in China or elsewhere.

Beginning in early 1940, however, its policy underwent
a subtle shift toward, but never all the way to, possible

American involvement in a war gainst Japan. In part, this
transition was due to the belief of Secretary Hull that an
embargo must be accompanied by other American measures in the
Far East. As early as February 1940, he indicated to Greene
that he would like to send the American navy to the Far East
before applying an embargo, but that the American public would
bitterly resist such action. Hull said that however unlikely
it might be that war with Japan would result from an embargo,
he felt the heavy responsibility for this decision resting
on him.[32]

Another factor influencing the committee to advocate
that the United States apply an embargo as part of a broader
policy was the advice of Henry L. Stimson, who for several
years had foreseen eventual war between the United States
and Japan. Harry Price recalls that during the first talk
with representatives of the committee in the fall of 1938,
Stimson jolted the delegation by saying: "I never imagined,
after the last world war, that we would be heading so soon
for another." When some one asked, "With Germany or Japan?"
Stimson further amazed them by answering, "Both."[33] Undoubtedly, Stimson encouraged the organization to look upon
the embargo as but one aspect of the impending confrontation
between the United States and Japan.

The committee never officially recommended that the
United States take military precautions in Asia, but it did
come to advocate a broader policy toward the Far East. In
its second main booklet *Shall America Stop Arming Japan?* it
outlined four elements of an enduring peace in Asia: the
ending of Japanese aggression, the restoration of an independent China, new and better machinery for peace, and the
development of economic cooperation.[34] But the booklet never

suggested any kind of American defense commitments in Asia;
in fact, Greene had eliminated a clause referring to "effective
guarantees of peace" for fear of antagonizing certain elements
within the committee and the public generally.[35]

In August 1940 Price's widely distributed essay "Pacific
Strategy" urged a similar policy including such elements as
increased aid to China, an understanding with Russia, a closer
accord with Australia, New Zealand and the Dutch and British
East Indies, and the ending of aid to Japan.[36] By a closer
accord with Australia and the Pacific islands, Price was
referring to such measures as trade agreements but never to
defense commitments. Arthur N. Young pointed out to Price:
"As to 'cutting off aid to Japan,' there is reason to favor
measures calculated to deter Japanese invasion of the Dutch
East Indies *before* having an oil embargo."[37] However, there
is no evidence to indicate that the committee ever spelled
out or supported such measures.

By this time, Roger Greene was unofficially advocating
fleet movements as a means of discouraging Japanese expansion.
On July 9, 1940, he sent a memorandum to Roosevelt, Hull and
others which recommended dispatching the Pacific fleet to the
Far East to dissuade Japan from attacking the Philippines,
Dutch East Indies or Singapore.[38] And in October he again
encouraged the government to send part of the Pacific fleet
to the western Pacific in order to check Japan.[39]

Admiral Yarnell also had been urging similar action.
In an address on August 24, 1940, he itemized what the United
States should do in the Far East: "As for China, we can stop
war materials going to Japan, insist on the opening of the
Burma Road, make the necessary loans to support the Nationalist
government and strengthen the Asiatic Fleet, basing the

reinforcements at Singapore." Yet, Yarnell apparently did not
visualize extensive American land forces in the Far East or
Europe: "Outside of garrisons for outlying and temporary
bases, we should not send troops in numbers outside of the
United States either to Europe or Asia."[40]

Statements such as these by Greene and Yarnell, however,
were never found within the official literature or correspondence
of the committee, partly for fear of antagonizing its more
anti-interventionist supporters, but primarily because few
of its members perceived a crucial connection between an
embargo and the possibility of war with Japan. In retrospect
and with the perspective of the postwar conflicts in Korea
and Vietnam, it is obvious that an embargo of war materials
and military intervention were complementary means of realizing
the same goal--an end to Japanese expansion. But, to Americans
of this period, these were two utterly different methods; one
spelled peace, the other spelled war. An embargo might seem
to be a warlike measure--the committee argued that it was not--
but at least it was not war itself. The contemporary idea of
the acceptable instruments of foreign policy possibly could
be expanded to include an embargo, but not military force.
Thus, the committee, as well as most of the American public,
could see no inconsistency, no evasion, in advocating that
the United States take economic measures to resist Japanese
expansion but refusing to recommend military action to reach
the same end.

Measured from the perspective of the present day,
the committee was asking relatively little of the United States
government. All that it demanded was that America cut off
its trade in war materials with a nation that was ruthlessly
invading a peaceful neighbor, and that was recognized by

many to be a potential threat to America itself. The group's
proposal might even appear to the modern observer to be grossly
inadequate; a concurrent advocacy of military precautions, if
not actual military intervention, would seem to have given
the committee a more realistic posture.

However, judged by the standards of its period, by
the prevailing conception of proper American involvement in
international affairs, the program of the committee was anything but conservative. To a generation indoctrinated in
the principle that moral force and public opinion were the
only legitimate tools for American diplomacy, the idea of
an economic embargo was seen as a radical departure. Before
criticizing the failure of the committee to recommend military
intervention in connection with its work, one must realize that,
as William L. Neumann emphasizes: "Americans who believed
that Japanese expansion could be checked only by force and
who favored using American force to this end constituted
a tiny minority throughout the 1930's, even to the day of
Pearl Harbor."[41] To advocate an embargo in 1938 was to place
oneself well in advance of the contemporary notion of the tech-
niques appropriate to American democracy; to advocate the use
of military force was to brand oneself a warmonger, unworthy
of serious attention. Seen in the context of its times, then,
the program of the group was both progressive and possible.

In its plea for limited American involvement in Far
Eastern affairs, for the United States taking "measures short
of war" to deter Japanese expansion, the committee played
a crucial part in the development of a more responsible view
of America's role in world affairs. With its program of
non-participation in Japanese aggression, it helped to rescue
many Americans from the false security of isolationism and

to set them on the road that was to lead to America's entrance
into the United Nations. The committeee did not deliver them
all the way or even most of the way to their destination,
but by starting them to think intelligently about the issues
that bound the future of America to that of distant lands, it
pointed clearly to the direction in which they must travel.

NOTES

Abbreviations Used in the Notes

AC   American Committee for Non-Participation in
      Japanese Aggression

HBP   Harry B. Price

RSG   Roger S. Greene

> Unless otherwise noted, the material cited
> below is part of the manuscript records of
> the American Committee for Non-Participation
> in Japanese Aggression at Littauer Center
> of Public Administration, Harvard University,
> Cambridge, Massachusetts.

Introduction

1. Information in this chapter relies heavily upon Selig
    Adler, *The Isolationist Impulse: Its Twentieth Century
    Reaction* (New York, 1957).

2. Wayne S. Cole, *America First: The Battle Against
    Intervention, 1940-1941* (Madison, Wisc., 1953).

1. Formation

1. Eliot Janeway, "Japan's Partner: Japanese Dependence
    Upon the United States," *Harpers Magazine*, 177:1-8
    (June 1938); Eliot Janeway, "Japan's New Need: American
    Steels, Machines and Oils," *Asia*, 38.6:338-341 (June 1938).

2. HBP to author, Mar. 13, 1967.

3. *Ibid.*, Jan. 23, 1967.

4. Report of Technical Committee on Ending American Aid
    to Japan, June 20, 1938.

5. HBP, Report on Trip to Washington, June 6-9, 1938.

6. *Ibid.*

7. Report of Perry and Wise, Inc., June 15, 1938.

8. *America's Share in Japan's War Guilt* (New York,
    July 1938), p. 78.

9. AC, *Progress and Program of the American Committee for Non-
    Participation in Japanese Aggression* (New York, Feb.
    16, 1940), p. 2; Edgar H. Rue to E. Snell Hall,
    Sept. 9, 1938.

10. Frank W. Price to author, Dec. 28, 1966.

11. HBP to author, Jan. 23, 1967

12. Minutes of National Board Meeting, July 27, 1938.

13. AC Press Release, January 19, 1939.

14. Minutes of National Board meeting, Sept. 16, 1938.

15. RSG to Abraham Flexner, Feb. 13, 1939.

16. HBP to Henry L. Stimson, Dec. 16, 1938.

17. AC Press Release, Jan. 19, 1939.

II. Organization and Campaign

1. Thomas A. Bisson to author, Jan. 9, 1967.

2. Elting E. Morison, *Turmoil and Tradition: A Study of the Life and Times of Henry L. Stimson* (Boston, 1960), pp. 468-476.

3. Frederick V. Field to HBP, Sept. 28, 1938-Oct. 4, 1940.

4. RSG to E. Snell Hall, Oct. 2, 1940.

5. AC, *Progress and Program*, p. 7. Information from this report was used throughout this chapter.

6. HBP to RSG, Dec. 28, 1938.

7. Minutes of National Board meeting, Jan. 3, 1940.

8. RSG to HBP, Jan. 6, 1940.

9. HBP to E. Snell Hall, Feb. 8, 1940.

10. Interview with HBP, New York City, Feb. 10-11, 1967.

11. *Ibid.*

12. RSG to HBP, Feb. 6, 1940.

13. HBP to Henry L. Stimson, Apr. 25, 1940.

14. RSG to HBP, Dec. 21, 1938.

15. HBP to author, Jan. 23, 1967; HBP to Henry L. Stimson, Apr. 25, 1940.

16. RSG to Mrs. John P. Welling, May 24, 1940.

17. RSG to Edward C. Carter, July 21, 1940.

18. HBP to E. Snell Hall, Aug. 25, 1939.

19. RSG to HBP, Aug. 5, 1939.

20. HBP to RSG, Aug. 15, 1939.

21. AC, Brief Report on Progress, Mar. 7, 1939.

22. HBP to Walter H. Judd, Nov. 26, 1938.

23. RSG to Alfred D. Heininger, Jan. 18, 1940.

24. RSG to Mrs. John Exter, May 31, 1940.

25. AC, *America's Share*, pp. 77-78.

26. Walter H. Judd to author, Dec. 28, 1966.

27. John W. Masland, "Missionary Influence Upon American Far Eastern Policy," *Pacific Historical Review*, 10.3:295 (September 1941).

28. AC, Statements of Income and Expenses to Mar. 23, 1942.

29. Interview with HBP, New York City, July 15, 1967.

30. AC, Statements of Income and Expenses to Mar. 23, 1942.

III. <u>Policy</u>

1. AC, *America's Share*, p. 78.

2. Walter H. Judd to author, Dec. 28, 1966.

3. HBP to RSG, Aug. 15, 1939.

4. Report of Technical Committee on Ending American Aid to Japan, June 20, 1938.

5. AC, *America's Share*, p. 77.

6. Maxwell S. Stewart to HBP, Jan. 11, 1939.

7. RSG to HBP, Jan. 12, 1939.

8. Minutes of National Board meeting, Jan. 3, 1940.

9. AC, "To Our Friends and Supporters," Mar. 15, 1940.

10. H.B. Bradford, quoted in AC, *America's Share*, p. 45.

11. AC, "Commentary on Recent Developments," Aug. 29, 1939.

12. AC, "War in Europe-- What About Asia?" Sept. 14, 1939.

13. HBP to A. Lawrence Lowell, July 27, 1940.

14. A. Lawrence Lowell to HBP, July 31, 1940.

15. Edgar H. Rue to E. Snell Hall, Sept. 9, 1938.

16. AC, *America's Share*, pp. 15-16.

17. AC, "To Friends and Supporters," Nov. 30, 1939.

18. AC, *America Supports Japanese Aggression* (New York, n.d.); AC, *Shall America Stop Arming Japan?* (New York, Apr. 15, 1940), p. 37. Information from both of these sources was used in this and the next three paragraphs.

19. HBP to Henry L. Stimson, May 29, 1940; AC, "To All Cooperating Groups," May 31,1940.

20. RSG to Cordell Hull, May 17, 1940.

21. Pearl Buck to HBP, Nov. 8, 1939.

22. HBP to Pearl Buck, Nov. 12, 1939.

23. HBP to Henry L. Stimson, Apr. 25, 1940.

24. RSG to Cordell Hull, May 17, 1940.

25. Edward H. Hume to HBP, Apr. 8, 1939.

26. RSG to Mabel C. Gage, July 27, 1940.

27. Herbert Feis, *The Road to Pearl Harbor: The Coming of the War Between the United States and Japan* (Princeton, N.J., 1950), p. 72.

28. RSG to C.M. Wesson, May 21, 1940.

29. AC, *America's Share*, p. 18.

30. HBP, "Our Far Eastern Policy, " *New World*, 2.9:5 (December 1939).

31. Henry L. Stimson, quoted in *New York Times*, Jan. 11, 1940, reprinted by AC.

32. AC, *Shall America*, p. 15.

33. *Ibid.*, p. 13.

34. AC, "To Our Friends," July 17, 1940.

35. Harry E. Yarnell, "The American Stake in the Pacific" (n.d.).

36. AC Press Release, May 15, 1940.

37. HBP to RSG, May 26, 1939.

38. AC, *America Supports Japanese Aggression.*

39. AC Press Release, Feb. 13, 1940.

40. AC, *America's Share*, p. 17.

41. AC, *America Supports Japanese Aggression.*

42. AC, *Shall America*, p. 29.

43. *Ibid.*

44. AC, *The Far Eastern Conflict and American Cotton* (New York, n.d.), *passim*.

45. AC, *Shall America*, p. 29.

46. AC, *America's Share*, p. 4.

47. HBP, "Pacific Strategy: A Key to American Defense" (n.d.), p. 23.

48. HBP, "Pacific Strategy," pp. 11-19.

49. AC, *America's Share*, p. 25.

50. *Ibid.*

51. AC, *Shall America*, pp. 11-13.

52. AC, "To Chinese Friends Who Wish to Cooperate with the American Committee," June 2, 1939.

53. AC, *America's Share*, p. 4.

IV. Opposition

1. Walter H. Judd, quoted in Minutes of National Board meeting, Jan. 3, 1940.

2. Kenneth Scott Latourette to RSG, Mar. 12, 1940.

3. AC, *America's Share*, p. 20.

4. Henry H. Douglas, "A Bit of American History--Successful Embargo Against Japan in 1918," *Amerasia*, 4.6:258-260 (August 1940).

5. AC, *America Supports Japanese Aggression.*

6. RSG to Lewis B. Schwellenbach, Feb. 21, 1940.

7. AC, *America Supports Japanese Aggression.*

8. Comments by Thomas A. Bisson, Feb. 21, 1940.

9. RSG, Memorandum for the Federal Council of Churches, Dec. 15, 1939.

10. RSG to Lewis B. Schwellenbach, Feb. 21, 1940.

11. RSG to Joseph C. Grew, Sept. 13, 1939.

12. RSG to Lewis B. Schwellenbach, Feb. 21, 1940.

13. *Ibid.*

14. RSG to Paul B. Jones, Apr. 17, 1940.

15. AC, *America's Share,* pp. 20-21.

16. RSG, Memorandum for the Federal Council of Churches, Dec. 15, 1939.

17. Walter H. Judd, quoted in *Hearings,* Senate Committee on Foreign Relations, 76th Congress, 1st Session, on Neutrality, Apr. 25, 1939 (Washington, D.C., 1939), p. 312.

18. RSG to Kenneth Scott Latourette, Mar. 11, 1940.

19. AC, *Shall America,* p. 34.

20. *Ibid.*

21. Eugene Staley, quoted in Report of Technical Committee, June 20, 1938.

22. AC, *America's Share,* p. 22.

23. RSG to HBP, Aug. 30, 1938.

24. E.W. Luccock, quoted in *America's Share,* p. 38.

25. RSG to Kenneth Scott Latourette, Feb. 29, 1940.

26. AC, *Shall America,* p. 3.

27. HBP, "Pacific Strategy," p. 4.

28. Report on the Attitudes of the Press, Apr. 7, 1939.

29. AC, *America's Share,* p. 23.

30. Report of Motorcade to Washington to Ask Congress to Stop the Shipment of War Supplies to Japan, July 13-22, 1939.

31. Evans F. Carlson, Outline of Talk Given in Washington, D.C., Feb. 27, 1940.

32. HBP, "Pacific Strategy," p. 15.

33. Dorothy Borg, *The United States and the Far Eastern Crisis of 1933-1938* (Cambridge, Mass., 1964), p. 234.

34. Tang Tsou, *America's Failure in China, 1941-1950* (Chicago, 1963), pp. 219-236.

35. *Ibid.*, pp. 134-138.

36. Edward H. Hume to HBP, Jan. 16, 1940.

37. HBP, Interview I.

38. Thomas A. Bisson to author, Jan. 9, 1967.

39. Report of Motorcade to Washington, July 13-22, 1939.

40. RSG to Cordell Hull, Feb. 20, 1940.

41. Paul V. Bacon to RSG, Mar. 11, 1940.

42. RSG to Paul V. Bacon, Apr. 4, 1940.

43. HBP to Henry L. Stimson, Aug. 3, 1939.

44. *Ibid.*, Apr. 25, 1940.

45. Adler, pp. 246, 257.

46. Feis, pp. 106-107.

V. Support

1. "Other Organizations and Their Relationship to AC" (n.d.).

2. HBP to C.H. French, Nov. 25, 1939.

3. RSG, Fund-raising letter, Mar. 3, 1939.

4. Frederick C. McKee to HBP, Apr. 29, 1940.

5. AC, *America's Share*, p. 75.

6. HBP to John D. Rockefeller, Jr., Sept. 1, 1938.

7. HBP to Henry L. Stimson, Dec. 16, 1938.

8. Ernest T. Weir to RSG, Nov. 6, 1939.

9. RSG to John D. Rockefeller, Jr., Jan. 24, 1939.

10. Resolution of Chamber of Commerce of the United States, quoted by AC, "National and Regional Groups and Organizations Protesting Aid to Japan," May 8, 1940.

11. HBP to RSG, May 26, 1939.

12. Paul V. Bacon to RSG, Mar. 11, 1940.

13. RSG to Paul V. Bacon, Apr. 4, 1940.

14. Charles Moser, quoted by HBP, Report on Trip to Washington, June 6-9, 1938.

15. Anonymous businessman, quoted by Charles Moser, quoted by HBP, Report on Trip to Washington, June 6-9, 1938.

16. R.E. McMath to Frederick C. McKee, Oct. 21, 1938.

17. RSG to John D. Rockefeller, Jr., Jan. 24, 1939.

18. AC, *Shall America*, p. 31.

19. William Green, President of A.F.L., quoted in AC, *America's Share*, pp.44-45.

20. Resolution passed by Industrial Council of C.I.O., quoted in AC, *America's Share*, p. 56.

21. Resolution presented by National Maritime Union of America to C.I.O. conference, quoted in AC, *America's Share*, pp. 52-53.

22. William Green to HBP, Sept. 28, 1938; John L. Lewis to HBP, Sept. 26, 1938.

23. James B. Carey to M. McBride, May 3, 1939.

24. Robert J. Watt to Pauline Mandigo, Apr. 27, 1939.

25. William Green to HBP, Nov. 27, 1939; John L. Lewis to HBP, Oct. 27, 1939.

26. HBP to RSG, Oct. 28, 1939.

27. "Local Labor Unions Protesting Aid to Japan" (n.d.).

28. Report on the Attitudes of the Press, Apr. 7, 1939.

29. *Ibid.*

30. Study of American Editorial Opinion on Far Eastern Policy, December 1940.

31. American Editors Discuss the Possibility of a Japanese-American War, December 1940.

32. Study of American Editorial Opinion on Far Eastern Policy, December 1940.

33. Paul A. Varg, *Missionaries, Chinese, and Diplomats: The American Protestant Missionary Movement in China, 1890-1952* (Princeton, N.J., 1958), p. 261.

34. James Claude Thomson, Jr., "Americans As Reformers in Kuomintang China, 1928-1937," Ph.D. thesis (Harvard, April 1961), pp. 405-411, pp. 427-428.

35. Varg, p. 251.

36. Varg, pp. 251-261; Masland, pp. 285-292.

37. HBP, Special and Urgent Letter to Missionaries from China, Dec. 9, 1939.

38. Varg, pp. 263-266; Masland, pp. 290-291.

39. Samuel McCrea Cavert, quoted in Confidential Notes of Luncheon Given by the Hon. Henry L. Stimson, Nov. 9, 1939.

40. Varg, p. 266.

41. Varg, p. 267.

42. Varg, p. 272; Cole, p. 48.

43. Masland, p. 292.

44. Varg, p. 268.

45. Walter H. Judd, quoted in Minutes of National Board meeting, Jan. 3, 1940.

46. Varg, pp. 268-269.

47. A.L. Warnshuis to HBP, May 29, 1939.

48. Resolution of Federal Council of Churches, quoted in AC, "National and Regional Groups and Organizations," May 8, 1940.

49. Elizabeth Rugh Price, "Leadership of Federal Council of Churches," Jan. 2, 1940.

50. Walter H. Judd, quoted in Minutes of National Board meeting, Jan. 3, 1940.

51. HBP, "Special and Urgent Letter to Missionaries from China," Dec. 9, 1939.

52. Varg, p. 271.

53. Resolutions passed by World Alliance for International Friendship Through the Churches, General Conference of Methodist Episcopal Church, South, and National Conference of Y.M.C.A.--all quoted in AC, *America's Share*, pp. 39, 49, 51; resolution passed by General Assembly of Presbyterian Church in U.S., quoted in AC, "National and Regional Groups," May 8, 1940.

54. "Other Organizations and Their Relationship to AC" (n.d.).

VI. <u>Termination</u>

1. Minutes of National Board meeting, June 3, 1940.

2. HBP to Henry Luce, June 8, 1940.

3. HBP to RSG, June 15, 1940.

4. *Ibid.*

5. Minutes of National Board meeting, Oct. 21, 1940.

6. HBP to author, Jan. 23, 1967.

7. AC, *America's Share,* p. 78.

8. Minutes of National Board meeting, Oct. 21, 1940.

9. HBP to author, Jan. 23, 1967.

10. Frederick V. Field to HBP, Nov. 11, 1940.

11. RSG to HBP, Dec. 12, 1940.

12. Minutes of National Board meeting, Oct. 21, 1940.

13. HBP to Frederick C. McKee, July 4, 1940.

14. HBP to Sidney Gamble, Jan. 6, 1941.

15. HBP to author, Jan. 23, 1967.

16. HBP to E. Snell Hall, Jan. 21, 1941.

17. Masland, p. 294.

18. HBP to author, Jan. 23, 1967; Card, Correspondence and Resource Files, February 1941.

19. HBP to author, Mar. 13, 1967.

20. RSG to Russell S. Codman, July 2, 1940.

21. William E. Dougherty, "China's Official Publicity in the United States," *Public Opinion Quarterly,* 6:73-74 (Spring 1942).

22. Interview with B.A. Garside, New York City, July 16, 1967.

23. Roy Y. Koen, *The China Lobby in American Politics* (New York, 1960), p. 99.

24. Varg, p. 294.

25. Walter H. Judd to author, Dec. 28, 1966.

26. Koen, p. 57.

27. Koen, p. 59.

28. Earl Latham, *The Communist Controversy in Washington from the New Deal to McCarthy* (Cambridge, Mass., 1966), pp. 203-216.

29. Latham, p. 251.

30. Koen, pp. 194-150.

31. T.A. Bisson to author, June 30, 1967.

VII. Evaluation

1. HBP to author, Jan. 23, 1967.

2. HBP, Report on Trip to Washington, June 6-9, 1938.

3. Results of American Institute of Public Opinion polls, quoted in Harold R. Isaacs, *Images of Asia: American Views of China and India* (New York, 1962), p. 173.

4. Results of American Institute of Public Opinion polls, quoted in Isaacs, p. 173.

5. Results of Public Opinion Survey Conducted by American Institute of Public Opinion, Aug. 30, 1939, reprinted by AC.

6. AC, *Progress and Program*, p. 8.

7. *Ibid.*

8. Masland, "Missionary Influence," p. 294.

9. William L. Langer and Everett S. Gleason, *The Undeclared War, 1940-1941* (New York, 1953), p. 42; Adler, p. 289.

10. Report of Motorcade to Washington, July 13-22, 1939.

11. Alexander DeConde, "On Twentieth-Century Isolationism," *Isolation and Security*, ed. Alexander deConde (Durham, N.C., 1957), pp. 15-16.

12. Adler, p. 289.

13. DeConde, p. 15.

14. Adler, p. 289.

15. HBP to E. Snell Hall, Sept. 1, 1942.

16. HBP to author, Jan. 23, 1967.

17. Adler, pp. 253-254.

18. Ralph Waldo Emerson, quoted by Adler, p. 254.

19. AC, *America's Share*, p. 24.

20. *Ibid.*, cover.

21. "Tentative Proposed Program Looking Toward Possible
     Action in Relation to the Sino-Japanese Conflict," May
     27, 1938.

22. Adler, p. 256.

23. AC, *America's Share*, p. 3.

24. RSG, Fund-raising letter, Dec. 4, 1939.

25. Adler, pp. 256-257.

26. Walter H. Judd, quoted in *Hearings*, Senate Committee
     on Foreign Relations, 76th Congress, 1st Session, on
     Neutrality, April 25, 1939, pp. 312, 316.

27. George F. Kennan, *American Diplomacy, 1900-1950*
     (Chicago, 1951), p. 49.

28. A.L. Warnshuis to HBP, May 29, 1939.

29. Adler, p. 282.

30. HBP to A.L. Warnshuis, May 31, 1939.

31. AC, *America Supports Japanese Aggression.*

32. RSG to HBP, Feb. 6, 1940.

33. Henry L. Stimson, quoted by HBP to author, Jan. 23, 1967.

34. AC, *Shall America*, pp. 38-39.

35. RSG to HBP, Apr. 7, 1940.

36. HBP, "Pacific Strategy," pp. 11-19.

37. Arthur N. Young to HBP, Sept. 1, 1940.

38. RSG, memorandum to Franklin D. Roosevelt, Cordell Hull,
     Frank Knox, Henry L. Stimson and Henry Morgenthau,
     July 9, 1940.

39. RSG, memorandum: How a Strong American Policy in the
     Far East Could Help Britain, Oct. 22, 1940.

40. Harry E. Yarnell, Address Given at Second Naval District
     Reunion, Aug. 24, 1940.

41. William L. Neumann, "Ambiguity and Ambivalence in Ideas
     of National Interest in Asia," *Isolation and Security*,
     ed. DeConde (Durham, N.C., 1957), p. 151.

BIBLIOGRAPHY

Manuscripts

This study is based primarily upon an examination of the manuscript records of the American Committee for Non-Participation in Japanese Aggression at Littauer Center of Public Administration, Harvard University, Cambridge, Massachusetts. This collection consists of sixteen unnumbered file cabinet drawers divided into three sections: the Correspondence File in ten drawers contains all correspondence of the New York headquarters, except for business correspondence; the Administration File in two drawers contains business correspondence, correspondence of the Washington office, and an incomplete collection of such records as minutes of National Board meetings, circular communications to Board members and sponsors, financial appeals, press releases, and studies of the research committee; the Resource Files in four drawers contain press clippings and articles relating to American non-participation in Japanese aggression.

Personal Interviews

Harry B. Price, New York City, February 10-11 and July 15, 1967.

B.A. Garside, New York City, July 16, 1967.

Personal Correspondence

Thomas A. Bisson, January 9, 1967 and June 30, 1967.

Walter H. Judd, December 28, 1966.

Frank W. Price, December 28, 1966.

Harry B. Price, January 23, 1967 and March 13, 1967.

Government Documents

Hearings, Senate Committee on Foreign Relations, 76th Congress, 1st Session, on Neutrality (Washington, D.C., 1939).

Published Sources

AC: American Committee for Non-Participation in Japanese Aggression, Publications:

America Supports Japanese Aggression (New York, n.d.).

America's Share in Japan's War Guilt (New York, July 1938). Available at Harvard College Library.

China Faces Japan—and America (New York, n.d.).

Christian Hands of America (New York, n.d.).

Far Eastern Conflict and American Cotton, The (New York, n.d.).

Japan's Partner: The U.S.A. (New York, n.d.).

Progress and Program of the American Committee for Non-Participation in Japanese Aggression (New York, Feb. 16, 1940). Available at Harvard College Library.

Shall America Stop Arming Japan? (New York, April 15, 1940). Available at Harvard College Library.

Suggestions for Committees Working to Stop the Arming of Japan (New York, n.d.).

What Can We Do to Stop America's Participation in Japanese Aggression? (New York, n.d.).

What One Person Can Do Toward Ending America's Arming of Japan (New York, n.d.).

Adler, Selig, *The Isolationist Impulse: Its Twentieth Century Reaction* (New York, 1957).

American Committee for Non-Participation in Japanese Aggression, see AC.

Borg, Dorothy, *The United States and the Far Eastern Crisis of 1933-1938* (Cambridge, Mass., 1964).

Cole, Wayne S., *America First: The Battle Against Intervention, 1940-1941* (Madison, Wisc., 1953).

DeConde, Alexander, "On Twentieth-Century Isolationism," *Isolation and Security,* ed. Alexander DeConde (Durham, N.C., 1957), pp. 3-32.

Dougherty, William E., "China's Official Publicity in the United States," *Public Opinion Quarterly,* 6:70-86 (Spring 1942).

Douglas, Henry H., "A Bit of American History--Successful Embargo Against Japan in 1918," *Amerasia,* 4.6:258-260 (August 1940).

Feis, Herbert, *The Road to Pearl Harbor: The Coming of the War Between the United States and Japan* (Princeton, N.J., 1950).

"Has America a Stake in the Far East?" *Town Meeting,* 4.16:1-48 (Feb. 27, 1939).

Isaacs, Harold R., *Images of Asia: American Views of China and India* (New York, 1962).

Janeway, Eliot, "Japan's New Need: American Steels, Machines and Oils," *Asia,* 38.6:338-341 (June 1938).

-----"Japan's Partner: Japanese Dependence Upon the United States," *Harpers Magazine,* 177:1-8 (June 1938).

Kennan, George F., *American Diplomacy, 1900-1950* (Chicago, 1951).

Koen, Roy Y., *The China Lobby in American Politics* (New York, 1960). Available in Harvard College Library.

Langer, William L., and Everett S. Gleason, *The Undeclared War, 1940-1941* (New York, 1953).

Latham, Earl, *The Communist Controversy in Washington From the New Deal to McCarthy* (Cambridge, Mass., 1966).

Masland, John W., "Missionary Influence Upon American Far Eastern Policy," *Pacific Historical Review,* 10.3:279-296 (September 1941).

Morison, Elting E., *Turmoil and Tradition: A Study of the Life and Times of Henry L. Stimson* (Boston, 1960).

Neumann, William L., "Ambiguity and Ambivalence in Ideas of National Interest in Asia," *Isolation and Security*, ed. Alexander DeConde (Durham, N.C., 1957), pp.133-158.

"Our Far Eastern Policy," *New World*, 2.9:5 (December 1939).

Price, Harry B., "Pacific Strategy: A Key to American Defense." Ms. distributed by Price in August and September, 1940, with a covering letter by Admiral Harry E. Yarnell.

Thomson, James Claude, Jr., "Americans As Reformers in Kuomintang China, 1928-1937," Ph.D. thesis (Harvard, April 1961).

Tsou, Tang, *America's Failure in China, 1941-1950* (Chicago, 1963).

Varg, Paul A., *Missionaries, Chinese, and Diplomats: The American Protestant Missionary Movement in China, 1890-1952* (Princeton, N.J., 1958).

INDEX

1. Liang Fang-chung, *The Single-Whip Method of Taxation in China*

2. Harold C. Hinton, *The Grain Tribute System of China (1845-1911)*

3. Ellsworth C. Carlson, *The Kaiping Mines (1877-1912)*

4. Chao Kuo-chün, *Agrarian Policies of Mainland China: A Documentary Study (1949-1956)*

5. Edgar Snow, *Random Notes on Red China (1936-1945)*

6. Edwin George Beal, Jr., *The Origin of Likin (1853-1864)*

7. Chao Kuo-chün, *Economic Planning and Organization in Mainland China: A Documentary Study (1949-1957)*

8. John K. Fairbank, *Ch'ing Documents: An Introductory Syllabus*

9. Helen Yin and Yi-chang Yin, *Economic Statistics of Mainland China (1949-1957)*

10. Wolfgang Franke, *The Reform and Abolition of the Traditional Chinese Examination System*

11. Albert Feuerwerker and S. Cheng, *Chinese Communist Studies of Modern Chinese History*

12. C. John Stanley, *Late Ch'ing Finance: Hu Kuang-yung As an Innovator*

13. S.M. Meng, *The Tsungli Yamen: Its Organization and Functions*

14. Ssu-yü Teng, *Historiography of the Taiping Rebellion*

15. Chun-Jo Liu, *Controversies in Modern Chinese Intellectual History: An Analytic Bibliography of Periodical Articles, Mainly of the May Fourth and Post-May Fourth Era*

16. Edward J.M. Rhoads, *The Chinese Red Army, 1927-1963: An Annotated Bibliography*

17. Andrew J. Nathan, *A History of the China International Famine Relief Commission*

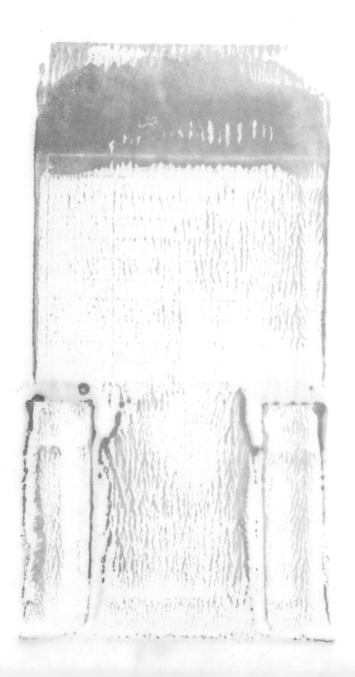